Living Unafraid

Living Unafraid

Lessons on Hope from 31 of the Bible's Most Loved Stories

Adam Hamilton

Convergent

New York

ISBN 978-1-5247-6052-6
Ebook ISBN 978-1-5247-6053-3

PRINTED IN THE UNITED STATES OF AMERICA

Book design by Andrea Lau

1 3 5 7 9 10 8 6 4 2

First Edition

CONTENTS

Contents

Contents

Contents

Living Unafraid

Our capacity to experience fear is a gift from God. Fear protects us from harm by preparing us to respond to perceived dangers or threats.

Often called the fight-or-flight mechanism, this "threat-detection system" is always switched on. And while it can be a gift that saves us when we're facing real danger, it often imagines a crisis where there is none or amplifies a minor threat to make it seem more serious or frightening than it really is. We worry about the future, about our health, about disappointing our friends and family. When these worries play over and over in our minds without resolution, it can rob us of life or keep us from doing things that would be life-giving.

Making matters worse, we are constantly bombarded with messages aimed at taking advantage of our fears. Politicians use fear to garner support for their candidacy or actions. Marketers can use fear to lead us to purchase their products. Twenty-four-hour news keeps us constantly aware of the most disconcerting things happening in the farthest corners of the world. Social media can leave us feeling anxious about our relationships or fearful that we're missing out, falling behind, or failing in life.

In my book *Unafraid: Living with Courage and Hope in Uncertain Times,* I discuss in detail why we fear the things we fear, and I offer ways we can press through the worries that most of us will face from time to time. I encourage the reader of this devotional to take a look at that book to delve into the causes of our fears and discover techniques for overcoming them. In that book, I used an acronym to outline four classic steps we can take to overcoming our fears:

Face your fears with a bias of hope.

Examine your fear-inducing assumptions in
   light of the facts.

Attack your anxieties with action.

Release your cares to God.

Long before people turned to therapists and medications for help with the things that made them anxious, they found peace and strength in their faith. The Bible records the experiences and reflections of those who trusted that God was with them, prayed for God's help, and found hope in God in the face of adversity and some of life's most frightening situations.

This thirty-one-day devotional is a companion to *Unafraid*. In it, I'll take you through many of the Bible's best-loved passages, exploring stories of people living with courage in the face of fear. After the first day's reading from Psalm 23, the daily readings start with the creation story in Genesis and progress through the entirety of scripture, concluding with the final chapters of Revelation.

Fear is a persistent topic in the Bible, mentioned more than four hundred times in one form or another. Over one hundred times the Bible tells us, "Don't be afraid." My hope in exploring these passages is to help you find hope, peace, and courage by realizing that if you struggle with fear, you are not alone; God is with you.

These daily readings are intentionally brief, in the hope that you might read them with a cup of coffee in the morning or as you lie down to sleep at night. My prayer is that in reading these devotions, you'll find help in releasing your cares to God, and that in doing this, you will experience comfort and peace.

Finally, a word about the real-life stories that appear in these devotionals. All are based on the actual experiences of people I have known and ministered with, though in most cases I've intentionally changed some details so that the individuals cannot be identified. In a few cases the stories involve a composite character, reflecting the experiences of several people with whom I've walked through similar circumstances.

Adam Hamilton
Spring 2019

I Will Fear No Evil

Yea, though I walk through the valley of the shadow
   of death,
I will fear no evil: for thou art with me.
   (Psalm 23:4 KJV)

pulled a chair next to her hospital bed and took her hand in mine. She'd been battling cancer for the better part of two years, and now her journey was nearing an end. She'd been amazingly strong throughout her treatment. Now she looked anxious. She asked me, "Adam, would you read me the words of the Twenty-third Psalm once more?" As I did, I invited her to say them with me:

The Lord *is* my shepherd; I shall not want. He maketh me to lie down in green pastures: he leadeth me beside the still waters. He restoreth my soul: he leadeth me in the paths of righteousness for his name's sake.

I could sense her mulling over each phrase as she repeated them out loud. She pictured Jesus standing by her, lovingly watching over her. She imagined the green pastures and the pond at her grandparents' home, where so many lovely childhood memories had been formed.

I told her how, on a recent trip to the Holy Land, some Bedouin shepherds invited me to join them as they drove their flock two hours into the desert. The entire journey, I was struck by how close the flock stayed to the shepherds. In that dry and barren land, the shepherds carefully led their flock to areas with vegetation and cisterns, drawing clean water for the sheep to drink. And if a sheep started to wander, at the sound of the shepherd's voice it would immediately run back.

"Yea, though I walk through the *valley of the shadow of death,* I will fear no evil," she continued, "*for thou art with me.*" Her words slowed, each one spoken with conviction, and the anxiety began to loosen from her eyes. "Thou art with me," she repeated.

As we prayed the psalm's final lines, "Surely goodness and mercy shall follow me all the days of my life: and I will dwell in the house of the Lord for ever," the woman remarked on how well those words described her life. "There has been pain, and sorrow, and some suffering," she said, "but through it all, I've felt his goodness and mercy with me." As I prepared to leave the hospital that day, the fear had vanished from the woman's face.

Psalm 23 has brought peace and comfort to people of faith for nearly three thousand years. It is a reminder of the many blessings in our lives, the moments when our hearts are full and our lives are overflowing with good things. And in times of pain, sorrow, and suffering, it is a reminder that God is our shepherd—that he is always with us, and because of this we do not need to be afraid.

I invite you to read the psalm aloud, making it your prayer for today. As you do, imagine God as your shepherd, and you his lamb whom he watches over, protects, and cares for.

The Lord is *my shepherd; I shall not want.*
He maketh me to lie down in green pastures:
he leadeth me beside the still waters.
He restoreth my soul:
he leadeth me in the paths of righteousness for his
name's sake.
Yea, though I walk through the valley of the shadow
of death,
I will fear no evil: for thou art with me;
thy rod and thy staff they comfort me.
Thou preparest a table before me in the presence of
mine enemies:

thou anointest my head with oil; my cup runneth over.
Surely goodness and mercy shall follow me all the days of my life:
and I will dwell in the house of the Lord for ever.
   (Psalm 23:1–6 KJV)

Exposed

During that day's cool evening breeze, [Adam and Eve] heard the sound of the Lord God walking in the garden; and the man and his wife hid themselves from the Lord God in the middle of the garden's trees. The Lord God called to the man and said to him, "Where are you?" The man replied, "I heard your sound in the garden; I was afraid because I was naked, and I hid myself." (Genesis 3:8–10)

Maggie, our family's beloved beagle, was a terrific dog who remained our companion for almost eighteen years. Like most beagles, she also had a great nose. One year, right after Halloween, that nose got her in trouble. My wife, LaVon, and I always buy a bit more candy than we'll need for trick-or-treaters, planning to enjoy it in the weeks that follow. (Peanut butter cups are our favorite.) After the last kids had rung our doorbell that night, we took the basket of candy and put it on the second shelf in our pantry.

You know where this is going, right? While we were at work the next day, Maggie pushed open the pantry door and somehow grabbed the basket from the second shelf. We came home to find a trail of candy wrappers strewn across the floor.

Maggie usually ran to meet us at the door, but that night there was no sign of her. Knowing that chocolate can be deadly for a dog, we began to shout, "Maggie!" But Maggie didn't come. We kept shouting and searching, worried that something had happened to her. That was when we noticed that there were wrappers in the bedroom, leading under the bed. When we looked under the bed, there she was. To our relief she did not appear to be sick, but she did look pretty guilty, tail tucked between her legs, aware that she'd done something she wasn't supposed to do.

Maggie's story reminds me of the first time fear shows up in the Bible. You likely know the story. God created Adam and Eve and gave them the Garden of Eden for their home. It was a beautiful place, lovely and safe, with the most wonderful things to see and eat. There was just one rule: Don't eat of the Tree of the Knowledge of Good and Evil.

But you know how that goes—tell someone not to eat something, and suddenly it becomes the one thing they most desperately want. So, with the help of the talking serpent, Adam and Eve convinced themselves that it was really okay to eat the forbidden fruit. They plucked and ate it. And immediately they understood that they'd made a mistake. Ashamed, and afraid of being caught and exposed, they tried to hide from God.

This is not simply the story of two people who lived ages ago. This is our story. Each of us has heard the serpent's whisper, calling us to do what we know we should not do. And when we succumb to temptation, the fear of getting caught usually comes next.

I wonder if you ever fear being exposed. It might be because of something you did that you knew was wrong, something that would lead to public embarrassment, or worse, if people found out. As a pastor for thirty years, I've heard many confessions—about things people sought God's forgiveness for, even if they were not ready to admit these things to anyone else. Here I've seen the truth behind the cliché "Confession is good for the soul." When we finally admit the wrong we've done and seek to make amends, fear often gives way to relief.

The Bible promises that God is "rich in mercy" and "abounding in steadfast love." The theologian Paul Tillich put it another way, saying that forgiveness is "God's answer to the questions implied by our existence." The preeminent sign of God's forgiveness was a cross, upon which Jesus hung, praying, "Father, forgive them, for they know not what they do."

God knows the skeletons in your closet. And confession *is* good for your soul. As you lay your burdens before God, take comfort in the words of the psalmist:

> *He does not deal with us according to our sins,*
> *   nor repay us according to our iniquities.*
> *For as high as the heavens are above the earth,*
> *   so great is his steadfast love toward those who*
> *   fear him;*
> *as far as the east is from the west,*
> *   so far does he remove our transgressions from us.*
>   (Psalm 103:10–12)

And Maggie? She survived her bout with peanut butter cups and never got into the candy again. (Although, in the course of her eighteen-year life, she got into plenty of other kinds of trouble.) For her, as with us, there was always grace.

We're all exposed before God. There are no secrets hidden from him. But God is even more ready to forgive you than you are to ask. So ask.

Lord, like Adam and Eve, I cannot hide from you. Forgive me, I pray, for the moments when I've succumbed to the serpent's whisper. Help me have the courage to make amends to those I've wronged. Wash me clean, make me new. Grant me your mercy and your peace. In Jesus's name, amen.

The Ark

The Lord saw that humanity had become
thoroughly evil on the earth and that every idea
their minds thought up was always completely evil.
The Lord regretted making human beings on the
earth, and he was heartbroken. . . . God said to
Noah, "The end has come for all creatures, since
they have filled the earth with violence. I am now
about to destroy them along with the earth, so make
a wooden ark." (Genesis 6:5–6, 13–14a)

Few biblical stories are better known than the story
of Noah's ark. God is heartbroken by the evil and
violence he sees humans inflicting upon one another and the earth. He purposes to put an end to it by
unleashing a flood of epic proportions, a kind of baptism of
the earth that will cleanse it from evil and start over again.

But before God does this, he notes that one man stands
out as being righteous, faithful, even blameless. His name

is Noah. So God plans to save Noah, his family, and the animals by calling Noah to build an ark—a giant floating box about 450 feet long, 75 feet wide, and 45 feet tall (a little more than half the length of the *Titanic*). The floods come, the waters rise, and all life on the planet is destroyed, except for the animals and people in the ark. Noah's obedience gives humanity another chance at life.

There are many ways in which this story might speak to us: the heartbreak of God concerning human violence; the faithfulness of Noah, even when God's call must have seemed absurd; God's promise that, whatever humans do, he will never again send a flood. But when early Christians looked at the story of Noah, they saw an additional truth. They saw the ark as a metaphor for the church. The church, in their view, was a kind of ship through which God provided shelter and salvation for the human race. They saw Jesus as its captain and taught that believers come to the ship, passing through the water of baptism, and ultimately find safety and respite from the storm. This imagery was so important that the place where the congregation sits in a church came to be known as the nave, from the Latin *navis,* which means ship. (Our word "navy" also comes from this same Latin word.)

Here's the part I want you to see: when the floodwaters rise in our lives, we often try to go it alone. But the church is intended to be one of the most powerful ways God carries us, speaks to us, and delivers us.

I think of a family who recently lost their daughter to suicide. The loss was devastating, but they told me how the members of their small group at church carried them through the intense grief and loss. I think of another family whose son I recently had the joy of baptizing—a little boy who was born with Down syndrome. This boy and his family have been surrounded by our ministry for children with special needs. Every week I see people like these gathered in worship, singing, praying, and listening as they find comfort and hope. In the church, each of these people found an ark to shelter them from the storms that had come to their lives.

Churches are not perfect. But here, too, the ark is a pretty good metaphor. I'm guessing the ark wasn't the most beautiful boat ever built. After all, Noah was a vine grower, not a shipbuilder. Likewise, I'm pretty sure the shipmates—Noah, his wife, and their sons and daughters-in-law—weren't perfect, either. (In fact, the saintly Noah later becomes the first man in the Bible to pass out drunk—and naked!) Frederick Buechner once said the church is like the ark because sometimes it "smells to high heaven" inside. But despite its shortcomings, it is "a ship to keep afloat, and like a beacon in the dark," it offers us hope of finding safe harbor.

God most often works to help us, speak to us, and save us through the people around us—through the ark that is the church. As Jesus noted, "For where two or three are gathered in my name, I'm there with them" (Matthew 18:20). We need the church, just as Noah needed the ark. For it is Christ's ship of salvation, and when we're with other believers who support and surround us, our fears don't seem quite so strong.

Do you have a church where you can find comfort, help, and companionship when the storms of life come your way?

Lord, when the floodwaters rise in my life, help me find safety in your lifeboat, the church. And when all is well in my life, help me hear your call, as a part of her crew, to rescue those being tossed by life's tempests. In Jesus's name, amen.

Leaving Home

The Lord said to Abram, "Leave your land, your
family, and your father's household for the land that
I will show you. I will make of you a great nation
and will bless you. I will make your name respected,
and you will be a blessing. I will bless those who
bless you, those who curse you I will curse; all the
families of the earth will be blessed because of you."
Abram left just as the Lord told him.
(Genesis 12:1–4a)

Abraham and Sarah were living a comfortable life
in the city of Haran, in what is today southeast
Turkey. He was seventy-five years old; she was ten
years younger. Haran was a thriving town within the Fertile Crescent, located on a major trade route linking the
empires of the east to the Mediterranean and Egypt.

But one day, Abraham (or Abram, as he was then
known) felt God saying, "Leave your land, your family,

and your father's household for the land that I will show you." I wonder how Abraham sensed God speaking to him. Did he hear an audible voice? Or did God speak to him in the way God usually speaks to us?

There have been many times in my life when I've felt God speaking to me. Yet I've never heard an audible voice or seen a vision of God. When I was sixteen, an older woman came up to me at church and said, "God has told me that you are supposed to be a pastor." When I asked her how God had said this to her, she said, "I just feel it in my heart." I told her I had other plans but was honored by her suggestion. A year later, after speaking at a church service, I myself felt this strong conviction that I was supposed to be a pastor. Just before I left for college, several people suggested that I was making a mistake; they said that I could have a wonderful career in business or politics or medicine. But I could not shake the feeling, the recurring thoughts of becoming a pastor.

Eight years later, the bishop of the United Methodist Church in Missouri told me that he and the district superintendents had discerned that God was calling me to start a new church. Once more, people I respected told me all the reasons why I should say no, the reasons the new church was destined to fail. But I could not shake the recurring dream, or the feeling that I was supposed to start a new congregation.

Both of those decisions entailed taking risks. Neither came with a guarantee that I or any of the others had actually, or accurately, heard God's will. And both decisions (not to mention a thousand other, smaller ones I've made across my life) came with sacrifices, plenty of fear, and a reasonable chance of failure. But how glad I am today that I said yes instead of no.

If you read the rest of Abraham's story in Genesis, you'll find that he experienced challenge after challenge in Canaan, and later in Egypt. But in the end, we tell his story today precisely because Abraham said that initial "Yes!" Abraham and Sarah were blessed, and ultimately, all the nations of the earth were blessed through them.

The challenge we have as human beings is that God *usually* speaks in a whisper instead of a shout. We sense God nudging us as we're reading scripture and the words seem to address our life situation. God whispers as we're listening to a sermon or a song, praying or meditating, and the message seems to strike a chord in our hearts. Other times, we hear God speaking through friends and family. But none of these are the "handwriting on the wall" or an audible voice that gives us certainty.

So we consider the calling in the light of scripture. We look for wisdom in the ministry and message of Jesus. We speak to others, inviting their wisdom and discernment on what we sense is God's call. We even carefully evaluate the message or calling with the help of our human faculties of reason. All of these factors help us discern whether the thoughts are coming from God.

Yet at the end of the day, Abraham's vision of the Promised Land was hardly logical. It seemed downright irrational to uproot his wife and servants and move to a foreign land with no clear destination in mind, a land where there might well be danger at every turn. Despite this, Abraham and Sarah went.

You, too, will be called, at times, to go to places you've never been, to take a leap of faith in response to little more than a whisper. Do what you can to test the call, examining and discerning its purpose in the light of scripture, with the help of trusted friends and by engaging your powers of reason. But know that sometimes we're called to go even when it doesn't make sense. If you've truly heard God's call, you'll find that God goes with you, blesses you, and makes you a blessing, just as God did with Abraham and Sarah.

Lord, help me listen for the promptings of your Spirit. Grant me discernment to know when it really is you calling. And help me to trust you, and to follow your call where you may lead me.

Wrestling with God

Jacob said, "O God of my father Abraham and God of my father Isaac . . . Deliver me, please, from the hand of my brother, from the hand of Esau, for I am afraid of him; he may come and kill us all, the mothers with the children." . . . The same night he got up and took his two wives, his two maids, and his eleven children, and crossed the ford of the Jabbok. He took them and sent them across the stream, and likewise everything that he had. Jacob was left alone; and a man wrestled with him until daybreak. (Genesis 32:9–11, 22–24 NRSV)

When you've done something underhanded, when you've deceived someone or taken something precious from them, a day of reckoning may come. The anticipation of that day, the unquenchable worry and fear, can often punish us more than the reckoning itself.

Jacob and Esau were twins, but Esau was born just a smidge before Jacob. This meant he was the firstborn, and *that* meant a birthright. As the oldest son, Esau would receive a double portion of the inheritance and become the head of the family after his father's death.

But Jacob was the smarter and more cunning of the two, and his mother favored him over her firstborn. One day, Jacob caught Esau at a weak moment, when the older brother was famished after a hard day's work, and coaxed him into selling his birthright for a bowl of stew. But the real cunning came later, when Isaac, the boys' father, was nearing death. Knowing that Isaac was virtually blind, Jacob's mother prompted him to pretend to be Esau and steal Isaac's blessing. Isaac proceeded to lay his hand on what he thought was Esau's head and, without realizing what he was doing, pronounced the blessing that was meant for the older son upon the younger. Now it was official. The birthright would go to Jacob.

When Esau found out what happened, he set out to kill his younger brother. Jacob fled. He went into hiding and spent years building his family and his wealth in a foreign land. But eventually, Jacob knew, he would need to go back to Canaan, for it was the land of promise. And that meant he would have to face the man he had swindled, the brother who wanted to kill him.

I wonder if you've ever done anything so hurtful to

someone else that you did everything in your power to avoid seeing them ever again. I think of a woman I know who, driving under the influence, crossed the median and struck another vehicle, killing a father and his young child. I think of a man who cheated on his wife with her best friend. Or the investment adviser who swindled his clients out of hundreds of thousands of dollars. Each had caused great pain to others, and all were afraid to face the people they had wronged.

In Jacob's case, he hoped that the years would have lessened the anger of his brother. But the closer he got to returning home, the more fearful he became. He sent ahead peace offerings of livestock, trying to pacify Esau's anger. But on the night before he entered Canaan, Jacob's anxiety rose. As he prayed in anguish, God came to him.

The way the story is told in the Hebrew of Genesis 32:22–32 is a bit mysterious. Jacob is said to wrestle with a man all night long. Yet by morning, if not long before, Jacob realizes that he's wrestling with God. I wonder, however, if Jacob wasn't also, in a sense, wrestling with himself—with the kind of man he had been, and the kind of man he would become.

Have you ever wrestled with God? I have, during seasons when I wondered if I'd failed God, or when I felt that God was failing me. I have prayed from a place of hurt or frustration, sometimes flat on my face in the darkness and sometimes shouting my questions to God on long walks. Was I wrestling with God in those moments? Or was God letting me vent until I finally realized I was wrestling with myself?

Read the Psalms and you'll find that a large number of them are laments—complaint songs capturing the psalmists' thoughts as they wrestle with God. There is something powerful about putting our questions, disappointments, or doubts before our Maker. While we're wrestling, we refuse to let go of God. We insist, as Jacob did, on God's blessing. And we find, to our surprise and joy, that when we refuse to let go, God's mercy and grace eventually come.

After his night of wrestling with God, Jacob awoke the next morning a different man. And when he finally met his brother face-to-face, he found a remarkable display of grace. To his surprise, Esau accepted his heartfelt confession and his attempt to make amends.

Is there someone in your life you have wronged, someone you have yet to reach out to and make amends? Perhaps you fear what might happen if you do. Jacob was afraid and, as a result, was forced to wrestle with the man he'd been, the man he would become, and the God in whom he trusted. It was in the wrestling that Jacob found the courage and determination to do what he knew God was calling him to do.

Thank you for allowing me to wrestle with you when I'm confused, angry, or just afraid. Help me to hold fast to you, to seek your blessing and not turn away from you. Help me to ask forgiveness, and to forgive. Place on my heart those I need to be reconciled to, and guide me as I seek to make amends. Amen.

From Prisoner to Prime Minister

When Joseph reached his brothers, they stripped off Joseph's long robe, took him, and threw him into the cistern, an empty cistern with no water in it. When they sat down to eat, they looked up and saw a caravan of Ishmaelites coming from Gilead. . . . Judah said to his brothers, "What do we gain if we kill our brother and hide his blood? Come on, let's sell him to the Ishmaelites." (Genesis 37:23–27)

[Years later, Joseph's brothers said], "What if Joseph bears a grudge against us, and wants to pay us back seriously for all of the terrible things we did to him?" . . . But Joseph said to them, "Don't be afraid. Am I God? You planned something bad for me, but God produced something good from it, in order to save the lives of many people, just as he's doing today. Now, don't be afraid. I will take care of you and your children." (Genesis 50:15, 19–21a)

J oseph was the eleventh son of Israel (Jacob), but unlike most younger sons at the time, Joseph was Israel's *favorite*. This became apparent one day when Jacob brought home a long, beautiful robe he'd had made just for Joseph. Resentment fermented in the hearts of Joseph's older brothers.

Then Joseph began having dreams that one day his brothers would bow down before him. Here's a bit of advice: if you have dreams that your siblings will one day bow down before you, whatever you do, *don't tell them!*

Unfortunately, Joseph did tell his siblings. And then one day when Joseph went out to the fields to meet up with his brothers where they were grazing the flocks, they decided to kill him. First they dropped him down a dry cistern, intending to leave him to die. A short time later they had a better idea: let's sell him to a caravan of Ishmaelite slave traders!

But that was just the beginning of Joseph's troubles. The traders sold him to an Egyptian official named Potiphar. Joseph put his head down, trying to work hard for his master, but Potiphar's wife took an interest in him. When Joseph rejected her advances, she accused him of attempted rape, and Joseph was sent to prison. Joseph had fallen from the favored son of a successful herdsman in Canaan to a slave imprisoned in an Egyptian jail; his life had become a nightmare.

Stories like Joseph's happen in our day, too. For twenty-four years, Darryl Burton served time in the Missouri State Penitentiary for a murder he had not committed. Key evidence that would have proven his innocence was withheld by the prosecution. At first, he was bitter, angry with a system that had unjustly convicted him. But one day he wrote a letter to Jesus, saying, "Jesus, if you're real and help me get out of this place, not only will I serve you, but I'll tell the world about you." He began to pray for those who had testified against him and for those who had suppressed evidence that would have proven he was innocent. His bitterness eventually began to fade, replaced by mercy and compassion.

Perhaps you've been rejected by family or friends, sold out, mistreated, or accused of things you haven't done. Maybe you've known the pain of repeated injustice and, perhaps, the fear that your life will never get any better— that you are destined to suffer forever.

I'm guessing that Joseph knew moments of anxiety, fear, and despair as he sat in his Egyptian prison. He had to have cried out, like the psalmist, "How long, O Lord? Will you forget me forever?"

Yet despite this, Joseph continued to trust God and sought to do "the next right thing." Genesis records that in prison, "the Lord was with Joseph and remained loyal to him. He caused the jail's commander to think highly of Joseph." Joseph was given responsibility to supervise and care for his fellow prisoners, and his ability to interpret dreams ultimately brought him to Pharaoh, whose troubling dreams no one else could decipher. Joseph interpreted Pharaoh's dreams to be warnings about an impending famine. Pharaoh exonerated Joseph and appointed him to oversee preparations for the famine and the distribution of grain during the famine—something like a prime minister.

One day, Joseph's brothers came from the land of Canaan, where the famine had left them without grain, and knelt before Pharaoh's official, not realizing that he was the brother they had sold into slavery years before. In the end, Joseph forgave his brothers and saved his family, as well as the future of Israel, by providing not only grain but land in the fertile delta region of Egypt.

The story reaches a climax with Joseph's words to his brothers: "You planned something bad for me, but God produced something good from it." This is what God does with painful things in our lives.

Darryl Burton's case was eventually reviewed by the courts. Evidence that had originally been suppressed was admitted in court, and in 2008 Darryl was exonerated and released from prison. To fulfill the promise he'd made in his letter to Jesus, he enrolled in seminary and became ordained as a United Methodist pastor. He now serves as a congregational care pastor at the Church of the Resurrection and recently started Miracle of Innocence, a ministry for wrongly convicted inmates. Darryl is one of the most remarkable human beings you'll ever meet. He is a living example of the way God takes the painful things in our lives and brings something good and beautiful from them.*

Don't give up when your life seems to be on a steady downward spiral. So were Joseph's and Darryl's. Hold on, keep trusting, and continue to do what is right. God specializes in redeeming and producing good from our unjust suffering.

Lord, I believe that you bring good from the pain, adversity, and injustices of life. Help me to trust you in the difficult times, and to continue to do the "next right thing" even when others wrong me. I pray that you will take the hardships of my past and bring something beautiful and redemptive from them. Amen.

---

* You can learn more about Darryl at darrylburton.org.

Please Send Someone Else

Moses was taking care of the flock for his father-in-law Jethro, Midian's priest. He led his flock out to the edge of the desert, and he came to God's mountain called Horeb. The Lord's messenger appeared to him in a flame of fire in the middle of a bush. . . . God called to him out of the bush, "Moses, Moses!" Moses said, "I'm here." . . . [God said,] "I'm sending you to Pharaoh to bring my people, the Israelites, out of Egypt." . . . But Moses said, "Please, my Lord, just send someone else." (Exodus 3:1–2, 4, 10; 4:13)

Have you ever been asked to do something that terrified you? Maybe it was a new job or a particular challenge at school. Or perhaps it was something you felt God calling you to do—a ministry, an act of service, a mission trip, or a complete career change. I have felt this fear on many occasions when I felt called by God—or was simply asked by others—to do something outside my comfort zone.

Moses grew up in Egypt; his birth led to the Bible's first adoption story. Given up by his mother in an effort to save his life, he was adopted by Pharaoh's daughter and raised in Pharaoh's house, as a prince of Egypt. But at the age of forty, he killed an Egyptian taskmaster who was beating Israelite slaves, and he was forced to flee Egypt. He landed in the vast desert of Sinai, where he married and began working as a shepherd, tending his father-in-law's flock.

Egyptians considered shepherds among the lowest rungs of the socioeconomic ladder—which meant Moses had gone from life at the top of the food chain to scrounging for a living at the bottom. As was the case with Joseph's story, God chose someone at the bottom for an important, world-changing task.

On this particular day, Moses was tending his flock when he saw a bush on fire, but not being consumed by the flames. Moses said to himself, "Let me check out this amazing sight and find out why the bush isn't burning up" (Exodus 3:3). In this one line we see an important key to the spiritual life: paying attention. God often seeks to speak to us in ways that we'll miss if we're not paying attention. We're meant to stay alert, to be curious, to spend time considering God's whisper or the convergence of events.

As Moses approached the bush for a closer look, God

spoke of his concern for the Israelites who were suffering under Egyptian bondage. And then God told the eighty-year-old Moses, "I want you to go back to Egypt, and to lead my people out of bondage."

The call was clear, but Moses was afraid. He had fled Egypt, a fugitive from the law. How could he go back? "Who am I to do this?" he objected. "I'm an eighty-year-old sheepherder."

God responded, "Yes, but I'll be with you."

"But what if the Israelites question me, asking who this God is that came to you in a burning bush?"

"Tell them, 'I Am Who I Am' sent me to you—the God of your ancestors, Abraham, Isaac, and Jacob."

"But what if they don't believe me or pay attention to me?"

"I'll give you a couple of demonstrations of my power."

"But, Lord, I can't speak well—I stutter."

"I'll help you speak!"

Finally, Moses blurted out in desperation, "Please, my Lord, just send someone else!"

How I love this story! So often, when we feel there's something we're meant to do, our fears immediately begin to shout. We can come up with any number of excuses for not responding to the call. And here's what's strange: God usually allows us to rationalize our way out of doing what-ever he was nudging us to do. But if Moses had walked away from the burning bush that day, content that he'd made a solid case for why God should find someone else, he would have missed the single greatest adventure of his life—an adventure in which God used him to liberate a people and form a nation.

The same is true for the tasks God puts in front of us. It might be volunteering to help teach children in Sunday school or serving the poor in your city. It might be public speaking or sharing your faith with someone else. It might be speaking up about an injustice you've witnessed or standing with others as they are harassed, picked on, or teased. Whatever it is that you've felt nudged by God to do, if you're human, you'll likely have no shortage of excellent excuses as to why you shouldn't do it—fears that begin to raise their voices in your head.

But the greatest adventures and the most meaningful moments in your life will come from saying yes to those promptings from God that scare you just a bit. As with Moses, God's response to your fears is simple: "Don't be afraid; I'll be with you."

Lord, you know how many times I've allowed my fears and excuses to keep me from pursuing things you've wanted me to do. Help me pay attention to the burning bushes in my life and grant me, I pray, the courage to say yes when I feel like saying no. In Jesus's name, amen.

Be Strong and Courageous

"As I was with Moses, so I will be with you; I will not fail you or forsake you. Be strong and courageous; for you shall put this people in possession of the land that I swore to their ancestors to give them. Only be strong and very courageous, being careful to act in accordance with all the law that my servant Moses commanded you; do not turn from it to the right hand or to the left, so that you may be successful wherever you go. . . . I hereby command you: Be strong and courageous; do not be frightened or dismayed, for the Lord your God is with you wherever you go." (Joshua 1:5–9 NRSV)

By Joshua 1:5, Moses was dead, and the mantle of leadership had fallen to his protégé, Joshua. The children of Israel were camped on the east side of the Jordan River, opposite the heavily fortified city of Jericho. In the book's opening words, God repeatedly said to Joshua, "Be strong and courageous."

Joshua was about to lead a ragtag band of former slaves and sheepherders into war. God had promised their ancestor Abraham that his descendants would one day possess this land. But as Joshua looked at the people around him and considered the fortified city of Jericho, with its massive walls, the chances of victory in battle seemed very small.

Much earlier in life, Joshua had entered the land of Canaan as a spy, exploring its walled cities. Of the twelve spies that surveyed the land, only he and Caleb believed the Israelites could take it. The other ten spies said that while it was a beautiful country, flowing with milk and honey, there was no way the Israelites could conquer it, for the people in the land were much larger and more powerful than the Israelites.

That had been nearly forty years earlier, but Joshua still remembered the cities and the men of large stature he'd seen when he'd snuck onto their land. Was Joshua, in fact, about to lead the Israelites on a march to their death as they crossed the Jordan River? Certainly some of their number would die in battle.

I recently visited the beaches of Normandy, where in June 1944 the Allied forces landed and began driving the Nazis to defeat. Standing at the Normandy American Cemetery, where nearly ninety-four hundred American soldiers are buried, I couldn't help but imagine the fear these men must have felt as their ships approached the landing beaches. Many of them were just eighteen or nineteen years old.

Some found strength in their belief that their lives belonged to God, and that death doesn't get the final word. Joseph Vaghi Jr. was among them. A Catholic officer, he led the men in his landing craft in the Lord's Prayer before they disembarked. He noted in an interview with the *Catholic Standard*, "When I went into Normandy, I had absolutely no fear, because I knew God would look after me. If he wanted me, that would be it."[*]

Not everyone can muster up such resolve in the face of fear, which is why Joshua needed to be en*couraged* by God on ancient Israel's D-day. And the courage and strength Joshua received would go on to inspire God's people to victory.

In *Unafraid*, I mention a definition of courage that has been helpful to me. It has been said in various ways by various people but is always some variation of "Courage is not the absence of fear but the willingness to do the right thing despite your fears."

Are you facing a battle that you know you must fight, a battle that God has called you to, but that leaves you truly

---

[*] Jerry Costello, "A D-Day Hero Who Put His Trust in God," *Catholic Standard*, June 5, 2013; https://cathstan.org/news/local/a-d-day-hero-who-put-his-trust-in-god.

afraid? If God has called you, then God goes with you. That doesn't mean the battle will be easy. It wasn't for Joshua, nor for the men who fought at Normandy. It does mean he's got a hold of you and will not let you go.

God's "pep talk" to Joshua, as he prepared to lead the Israelites into battle, involved two things: keeping God's commandments and remembering that God would be with him wherever he went. *"Do not turn from it to the right hand or to the left. . . . Be strong and courageous; do not be frightened or dismayed, for the Lord your God is with you wherever you go."*

Lord, there are many times when I am afraid. In my fear, help me not to turn away from your path but, rather, to walk in it each day. Help me find strength and courage by trusting that you are with me now and always. Amen.

Two Are Better Than One

"Don't urge me to abandon you, to turn back from following after you. Wherever you go, I will go; and wherever you stay, I will stay. Your people will be my people, and your God will be my God. Wherever you die, I will die, and there I will be buried. May the Lord do this to me and more so if even death separates me from you." (Ruth 1:16–17)

Many of the Bible's heroes knew their share of tragedy. The short narrative known as Ruth, one of only two biblical books named for women, tells such a story.

Naomi, her husband, Elimelech, and their two sons left Bethlehem during a famine, traveling east, across the Jordan River, where there was grain. They settled in Moab, and Naomi's two sons married Moabite women. But some time after they settled there, Elimelech died. Some time later, Naomi's sons died as well.

The loss of a spouse is hard enough, but to lose both of one's children? The grief must have been nearly too much to bear. Naomi would later change her name to Mara, which means "bitter." It is not hard to imagine why. The bitterness of her life could not help but leave a bitterness in her soul.

Naomi decided that the only thing left to do was to return to her hometown of Bethlehem, on the other side of the Jordan River from Moab. The famine was over, her homeland was fruitful once again, and she had land and family in Bethlehem. She encouraged her daughters-in-law to remain in Moab and remarry, and after many tears and embraces, she prepared to set off.

But Ruth, one of her daughters-in-law, insisted on going with Naomi, leaving her homeland in order to care for her mother-in-law in Israel. Listen to Ruth's request, some of the most memorable and beautiful words in scripture:

> "Don't urge me to abandon you, to turn back from following after you. Wherever you go, I will go; and wherever you stay, I will stay. Your people will be my people, and your God will be my God. Wherever you die, I will die, and there I will be buried. May the Lord do this to me and more so if even death separates me from you." (1:16–17)

This is astounding devotion. Ruth had decided that she would go to a land she had never been to before, leaving behind her own blood family. Whatever future Naomi faced back home, Ruth would face it with her.

The future Naomi faced, the future Ruth chose to face with her, included the poverty of a widow with no men to provide for her needs. (In a patriarchal society, it was the men who owned property and controlled wealth.) In addition, there was the threat of sexual harassment mentioned in Ruth 2:9 and 2:22, a threat toward which the younger Ruth was particularly vulnerable. Today, the #MeToo movement has drawn the world's attention to the issue of sexual harassment and sexual assault in many workplaces. Ruth is a reminder that objectification, harassment, and sexual assault have been a tragic part of life for women in every culture, race, and religion throughout history.

Ruth likely understood these possibilities, but she still chose to go with Naomi to Naomi's home country. As I read their story, I'm reminded of Ecclesiastes 4:9–12:

Two are better than one because they have a good return for their hard work. If either should fall, one can pick up the other. But how miserable are those who fall and don't have a companion to help them up! Also, if two lie down together, they can stay warm. But how can anyone stay warm alone? Also, one can be overpowered, but two together can put up resistance. A three-ply cord doesn't easily snap.

Friendship is a key to living with courage and hope. When life is unraveling for us, our first instinct is often to withdraw from others—this is what Naomi sought to do in sending her daughters-in-law away. But it is in moments like these, most of all, that we need to let others into our lives.

We'll all be Naomi at some point in our lives, in need of a Ruth. And each of us will be called to be a Ruth for someone else. It is in these kinds of relationships that we find we can bear our grief and sorrow, and see our bitterness turned to joy.

Is there someone you know right now walking through the bitterness of a Naomi who needs you to be their Ruth? Or perhaps you are walking in Naomi's shoes right now, and when others sought to help, you've pushed them away, as Naomi sought to do with her daughters-in-law. Is it time for you to allow others to come alongside you and, in the process, not only to find blessing in your life but to bless them as well?

Lord, help me to let others in when I'm struggling, depressed, or feeling alone. And help me watch for those in my life who may need me to be their Ruth. Make me a steadfast friend to others. Amen.

The Giants in Your Life

A champion named Goliath from Gath came out
from the Philistine camp. He was more than nine
feet tall. He had a bronze helmet on his head and
wore bronze scale-armor weighing one hundred
twenty-five pounds. He had bronze plates on his
shins, and a bronze scimitar hung on his back. His
spear shaft was as strong as the bar on a weaver's
loom, and its iron head weighed fifteen pounds.
(1 Samuel 17:4–7)

t's one of the great stories of the Bible. A young shepherd
boy, David, takes his slingshot and slays the Philistine
giant Goliath. The story has become a metaphor for
seemingly hopeless causes in life and the possibility that
giants can be defeated.

The Philistine army was camped on one side of the Valley of Elah, the Israelites' ragtag army on the other. When
Goliath, the Philistine champion, walked out onto the

battlefield, taller than Shaq and sporting some serious armor, he was terrifying. Then he opened his mouth and began taunting the Israelites, and their response was understandable: "When Saul and all Israel heard what the Philistine said, they were distressed and terrified."

We all face giants from time to time—seemingly impossible situations that leave us distressed. For one man I knew, it occurred at the height of the Great Recession, when his business failed. There seemed to be no way out. Even bankruptcy offered only limited help. And it wasn't just the loss of the business that terrified him. It was the embarrassment, the failure, the shame, and the loss of his identity. He felt his was a hopeless cause.

When we face frightening or disconcerting circumstances, we have a natural tendency to catastrophize. What a great word! Instead of conjuring up courage, the initial response of most people is to assume the worst—to see no way out. We hear the word "cancer" and assume we're going to die. We lose our job and we are certain no one will ever want to hire us again. Whatever the giant we're facing, our tendency is to assume we're defeated.

David, likely just a young teenager at the time of his greatest battle, didn't know that Goliath was invincible. Instead, he said to King Saul, "Don't let anyone lose courage because of this Philistine! I, your servant, will go out and fight him!" Amazingly, Saul let him go to fight the giant.

Goliath taunted David. "Come here," he said to David, "and I'll feed your flesh to the wild birds and the wild animals!" Listen to David's response: "You are coming against me with sword, spear, and scimitar, but I come against you in the name of the Lord of heavenly forces." Then, as the giant moved closer, David took a smooth stone from his bag, placed it in his slingshot, and slung it at the giant. A direct hit, right in the middle of Goliath's forehead, and the giant fell to the ground. David, who wasn't even carrying a sword, took Goliath's sword and finished him off!

There are two things we should consider from this story. The first is that while the rest of the Israelites were shaking with fear, and undoubtedly praying to God, David stepped out onto the battlefield with faith. He's a model of what Saint Benedict meant by his famous motto: *Ora et labora,* or "pray and work."

Fear is meant to move us to action. When we don't act, we get stuck in our fight-or-flight response, and anxiety builds and builds inside our hearts. We obsess, fixate, and become overwhelmed by our fears.

We're meant to pray *and* take action. But the action we take is done under the belief that "the Lord of heavenly forces" is by our side, and that he is able to "make a way where there seems to be no way." Whatever you are facing, know that there are no impossible situations with God. Even death itself has been defeated by him.

Remember the businessman I mentioned? He spent

two years struggling, feeling like throwing in the towel, wondering if the giant of economic disaster would destroy him. But through the tears, and through the fears, he refused to give up. He prayed and he worked, and one day the clouds began to part and the giant of financial disaster fell, and the businessman lived to tell about it. I see him every week at church, and he is a visible reminder to me of the importance of not being paralyzed by fear but, with faith, continuing to put one foot in front of the other, confident that God will see you through.

The Lord of heavenly forces is with *you*. And you can, with God's help, defeat the giants in your life. Don't give up. Keep praying, and don't forget your slingshot.

Lord, you know the giants I face. Help me remember that you are the Lord of heavenly forces, and that you are in my corner. Help me trust that no matter the odds, you can and will see me through. Amen.

Whom Shall I Fear?

The Lord is my light and my salvation—
   whom shall I fear?
The Lord is the stronghold of my life—
   of whom shall I be afraid? (Psalm 27:1 NIV)

Take a Bible and open to the very center. Unless your Bible has extensive notes and maps in the back, you'll find yourself somewhere in the Book of Psalms. I've always found this a helpful metaphor. At the heart of the Bible is a book that expresses the heart of God's people as they sing and pray during the various seasons of life.

Some psalms are exclamations of praise, written when something wonderful had just happened. But there are other seasons in life when exuberance is far from our hearts. Seasons of opposition or adversity. Times of hopelessness or despair. In these moments, we might be more inclined to cry out to God for help or to express our frustration and doubt. Consider Psalm 13: "How long, Lord? Will you forget me forever? How long will you hide your face from me? How long must I wrestle with my thoughts and day after day have sorrow in my heart?" (Psalm 13:1–2b NIV). Or the opening words of Psalm 22, which Jesus himself prayed from the cross: "My God, my God, why have you forsaken me?" (NIV).

These psalms are often called "psalms of lament" or, simply, "complaint psalms." I'm grateful that these prayers were included in the Bible. They are honest and gritty. They might even make us cringe a bit at their frank expressions of hurt and the longing for God to exact vengeance on the authors' enemies. (Like Psalm 137:9, which says to the Babylonians who destroyed Jerusalem and took the Jewish people captive, "Happy is the one who seizes your infants and dashes them against the rocks.") These verses express not the heart of God but the heart of people who have been hurt.

But while a prayer asking God to destroy the psalmists' enemies is occasionally found, what these psalms most often include are words that reaffirm a trust and confidence in God's ability to deliver the psalmist. Even when a psalm begins with a complaint, it nearly always ends with an affirmation, a reminder of what God has done to deliver the psalmist in the past or can do in the future to rescue the author from harm.

Psalm 13, which begins, as noted earlier, "How long, Lord? Will you forget me forever?" ends with this powerful prayer: "But I trust in your unfailing love; my heart rejoices in your salvation. I will sing the Lord's praise, for he has been good to me."

The overarching message of the Book of Psalms are these expressions of confidence and hope, like the opening words of this day's reading, from Psalm 27:1:

> *The Lord is my light and my salvation—*
> *whom shall I fear?*
> *The Lord is the stronghold of my life—*
> *of whom shall I be afraid?* (NIV)

Peter Böhler, an eighteenth-century Moravian missionary, once famously told the struggling John Wesley, "Preach faith till you have it; and then, because you have it, you will preach faith." Something important happens in our hearts when we speak aloud our trust in God. In some sense, this is what the psalmists were doing—singing about their trust in God until it eventually settled into their hearts. This is still true for us today.

Every day, I try to read and pray at least one psalm. I say its words aloud, then choose one or two verses to focus on and repeat in prayer. Some psalms speak deeply to me. In others, I have to work to find a verse or two that resonate. But more often than not there will be a phrase or two, sometimes more, that are exactly what my soul needs to hear in that moment.

These are but two examples of verses I prayed recently. Take a moment to pray them aloud, not once but several times, slowly speaking these words until their meaning moves from your lips to your heart.

When I am afraid, I put my trust in you.
 In God, whose word I praise—
in God I trust and am not afraid.
 What can mere mortals do to me?
  (Psalm 56:3–4 NIV)

But I will sing of your strength,
 in the morning I will sing of your love;
for you are my fortress,
 my refuge in times of trouble.
  (Psalm 59:16 NIV)

Missing Out

[Solomon] finished the temple in all its details and
measurements in the eleventh year during the eighth
month, the month of Bul. He built it in seven years.
Now as for Solomon's palace, it took thirteen years
for him to complete its construction.
(1 Kings 6:38–7:1)

As his reign came to a close, King David appointed
his son Solomon to rule as his successor. David
had been known for his prowess as a warrior, as
well as for his psalms. Solomon was known for his wisdom,
but as he amassed more power, he also became known for
his voracious appetite for more—more food, more chariots, more palaces, more wives, and more gold.

It was left to Solomon to build the temple that David
had hoped to build as a representation of God's earthly
dwelling place among his people. David provided the plans
and many of the resources for this magnificent structure.

Solomon conscripted the workers and made arrangements for its timbers and stone.

But after God's palace, the temple, was completed, the writer of 1 Kings offers a subtle clue that Solomon was not as wise as he seemed: Solomon completed the Lord's temple in seven years, but it took thirteen years to complete the construction of his own palace. If the length of time the construction required was any indication, Solomon's palace was the more palatial of the two.

The writer of 1 Kings goes on to tell us that Solomon amassed huge quantities of gold, along with fourteen hundred chariots and twelve thousand horses. And when it came to wives, Solomon had many hundreds. Who could possibly need fourteen hundred chariots and a thousand wives and concubines? What was up with Solomon?

In 2004, a name was given to this condition: FOMO, the fear of missing out. Fear of missing out is the motivation behind most midlife crises and the impulse that keeps us constantly checking our cell phones and social media. It's not just King Solomon who struggled with FOMO; it is a common fear many of us wrestle with.

Throughout most of the Bible's history, the book Ecclesiastes was thought to have been written by Solomon. Though this identification is questioned by some scholars today, whoever wrote Ecclesiastes definitely wrestled with FOMO. The author writes as an old man looking back over his life, describing his long quest for material satisfaction:

I acquired male servants and female servants . . . I also had great herds of cattle and sheep, more than any who preceded me in Jerusalem. I amassed silver and gold for myself, the treasures of kings and provinces. I acquired male and female singers for myself, along with every human luxury, treasure chests galore! So I became far greater than all who preceded me in Jerusalem. . . . I refrained from nothing that my eyes desired. I refused my heart no pleasure. (Ecclesiastes 2:7–9a, 10a)

Yet for all he acquired, the writer of Ecclesiastes remained unsatisfied. His constant refrain in the book is "meaningless, all is meaningless, a chasing after the wind." This points to a truth philosophers throughout history have recognized: the more we focus on satisfying our desire for pleasure, the less satisfied we become. Psychologists refer to this as "hedonic adaptation."

Jesus challenged FOMO and its assumption that "more + better = happiness" on many occasions. One thing he said that I've memorized and that I recite when I feel the urge to buy a new camera, watch, gadget, item of clothing, car, or something else are these words: "Watch out! Be on your guard against all kinds of greed; *life does not consist in an abundance of possessions*" (Luke 12:15, emphasis added).

How do we overcome FOMO and our constant desire for more? We cultivate and express gratitude for what we have, we nurture a heart and habit of generosity toward God and others, and we retrain our minds to understand that life is not found in an abundance of possessions.

I prepared the following prayer for a little book on finances I wrote several years ago. We gave it out as a prayer to our members, printed on a key-chain tag, and invited them to pray this prayer before they went shopping. I invite you to pray it aloud, *twice,* focusing on each word.

*Lord, help me to be grateful for what I have, to remember that I don't need most of what I want, and that joy is found in simplicity and generosity. Amen.**

---

* *Enough: Discovering Joy Through Simplicity and Generosity* (Nashville: Abingdon Press, 2009).

Praying to Die

Elijah was terrified. He got up and ran for his life. He arrived at Beer-sheba in Judah and left his assistant there. He himself went farther on into the desert a day's journey. He finally sat down under a solitary broom bush. He longed for his own death: "It's more than enough, Lord! Take my life because I'm no better than my ancestors." (1 Kings 19:2–4)

Elijah is one of the most revered prophets in scripture. He is one of only two people in the Bible who did not die but instead was taken up to heaven. Malachi, the last book of the Old Testament, foretold that Elijah would return before the coming of the "day of the Lord." To this day, Jews continue to await Elijah's coming and speak of it each Passover. In the New Testament, Jesus is seen speaking to Elijah on the Mount of Transfiguration.

Clearly Elijah was a man of deep faith, beloved by God.

Yet in 1 Kings 19, we find that Elijah was so depressed, so filled with despair, that he prayed for God to take his life. What could have led Elijah to such despair?

Elijah lived in the ninth century before Christ, a time when Israel was divided into two kingdoms. Ahab and Jezebel ruled as king and queen over the northern kingdom, Israel. Their reign was characterized by evil, injustice, and idolatry. God called Elijah to confront the king and queen, but other prophets who had opposed them had been put to death. After a dramatic confrontation with Jezebel's prophets atop Mount Carmel (see 1 Kings 18:18–46), Queen Jezebel swore that Elijah would be killed, too.

Elijah fled a hundred miles south to the Negev Desert, fearing for his life. But at some point, he began to fear something else. He was afraid that his life would never get better. He was tired of running, tired of the years of playing cat and mouse where he was the mouse and Ahab and Jezebel were the cats. He feared that his life would always feel as bleak as it felt in that moment. It was then that he "longed for his own death."

Over the years, I've cared for many people who related to Elijah, who prayed for and longed for death. I've also cared for many families whose loved ones did more than pray to die. They felt so hopeless, they attempted suicide, and in some cases, they completed it.

All of us know the feeling that things will never get better—a fear that the pain or emptiness or despair one is currently experiencing or the dire circumstances one is currently going through will never change. You may have thought, If I'm always going to feel this way, I don't want to go on. I can't go on.

But God refused to take Elijah's life. A premature death was not, and is not, the answer. Following his prayer, Elijah lay down and went to sleep. As he slept, a messenger* from God tapped him and said, "Get up! Eat something!" The messenger had a meal of bread and water prepared for Elijah. Elijah ate, then went back to sleep (which is often what we do when we're depressed). A short time later the messenger woke Elijah again and said, "Eat something, because you have a difficult road ahead of you" (1 Kings 19:7).

Note that the messenger didn't say, "God's going to fix it all real soon." No, the messenger said, "Eat something, because the journey ahead is not going to be easy."

Elijah ate and drank and then walked for forty days, until he reached Mount Horeb,† where he prayed, complaining to God. Eventually, Elijah felt God's presence, as the New International Version (NIV) describes it, in "a gentle whisper." God listened patiently to Elijah's com-

---

* Some translations say "angel," but the word simply means "messenger," as it is translated in the Common English Bible (CEB).

† At times in the Bible, Mount Horeb is synonymous with Mount Sinai.

plaints, then said, in essence, "Go back, Elijah, I have more for you to do."

Elijah returned to Israel, where he continued his important ministry working for justice and confronting evil. He mentored a young man to take his place—Elisha. Then one day God sent a chariot of fire to take Elijah directly to heaven. What Elijah would have missed had he died at Mount Horeb that day!

I recently saw a woman holding her granddaughter in her arms, with a look of sheer joy on her face. I was reminded of how, ten years earlier, this same woman had come to me praying to die. I think of the man whose financial failure left him wanting to "end it all" but who chose to keep going. A year later he began to slowly rebuild his career, and today he is like a completely different man, filled with hope and fulfilled by a job he loves.

There are countless other stories I could tell. They have filled me with the conviction that pain and darkness will not last forever. Get up and eat. Drink. Walk. Listen for the sound of the gentle whisper. Know that the Lord is with you, and that he's not done with you yet.

Lord, you know that there are times when I feel like giving up. And there are people I know who feel that way now. Help me to be still and know that you are God, that you are with me, and that you have plans to use even my pain for good. And make me a messenger to those who are struggling with

*darkness and despair. Use me to offer friendship, encourage-
ment, and care to them.*

If you or someone you know is feeling suicidal, you may
need more than a devotion and faith. The National Suicide
Prevention Lifeline is available twenty-four hours a day at
1-800-273-8255. The person on the other end of the line
may be God's messenger for you.

For I Am Your God

But now, says the Lord—
the one who created you, Jacob,
    the one who formed you, Israel:
Don't fear, for I have redeemed you;
    I have called you by name; you are mine.
When you pass through the waters, I will be
    with you;
        when through the rivers, they won't sweep
            over you.
When you walk through the fire, you won't be
    scorched
    and flame won't burn you.
I am the Lord your God,
    the holy one of Israel, your savior.
        (Isaiah 43:1–3a)

The Book of Isaiah is a fascinating, enigmatic, beautiful, and complicated text. Like those of many of the prophets, Isaiah's message was one that comforted the afflicted and afflicted the comfortable. In the early portions of the book, the words of warning (afflicting the comfortable) take precedence, sprinkled intermittently with words to comfort the afflicted. In the latter portions of the book, it is words of comfort for the afflicted that take center stage.

Isaiah denounced the injustice and misuse of power that were rampant among many of Israel's leaders, resulting in the rich getting richer and the poor getting poorer. He also decried the idolatry of those who claimed to serve God while their hearts worshipped wealth and power or they dabbled in the worship of the other ancient Near Eastern deities. These Isaiah sought to afflict. Yet throughout the book, and particularly in its later chapters, the author(s) of Isaiah sought to comfort the afflicted, promising that their sins would be forgiven and their oppression ended, and that everlasting joy would return to them.

Throughout history, Christians have found that Isaiah's words speak profoundly to us as well, sometimes afflicting, sometimes comforting us. Jesus and the New Testament authors quote or allude to Isaiah at least eighty-five times, finding new applications for the prophet's words. The same is true for Christians today as we read Isaiah.

While earlier sections of Isaiah seem written to warn of

judgment to come, the latter chapters of the book appear written to the Jewish people who had been crushed by the Babylonian Empire and taken from their homeland to live in Babylon.* Speaking to the exiles in Babylon, Isaiah promises a return from exile—a journey back to the land of Israel, though this journey would not be without its challenges. He writes on behalf of God:

> *When you pass through the waters, I will be with you;*
> *when through the rivers, they won't sweep over you.*
> *When you walk through the fire, you won't be scorched*
> *and flame won't burn you.* (Isaiah 43:2)

Their journey home might include floods and fire, but the floodwaters would not overwhelm them; the fire would not destroy them. How encouraging for that generation of exiles, many of whom had never been to the land of promise, to hear that no matter what, God would protect them and bring them back home.

Notice that God does not say, "*If* you pass through the floodwaters" or "*If* you walk through the fire." No, God says through Isaiah, "*When* you pass through the waters" and "*When* you walk through the fire." We will walk

---

* Much of Isaiah 1–39 is thought to have originated prior to or just after 701 BC, while much of Isaiah 40–66 addresses the situation of Jews living in exile in Babylon in the sixth century BC.

through floodwaters and fires in our lives. There will be adversity—that is part of life. But when we walk through these times of adversity, we don't have to fear. "I will be with you," God says. "Therefore, the waters and flames will not destroy you."

No matter what floods or fires you walk through in the coming year—illness, job loss, the loss of someone you love, financial distress, or literal floods or fires—God will be with you, and nothing will ultimately defeat you, for you are his and he's called you by name. Even death cannot ultimately defeat you, because, as we'll see in the chapters ahead, he has defeated even death itself.

Lord, thank you for redeeming me, for knowing my name, and for calling me your own. Help me to trust you when the floods and fires come. Help me to remember that you are always with me and to trust in your unfailing love.

I Know the Plans I Have for You

I know the plans I have in mind for you, declares the Lord; they are plans for peace, not disaster, to give you a future filled with hope. When you call me and come and pray to me, I will listen to you. When you search for me, yes, search for me with all your heart, you will find me. I will be present for you, declares the Lord, and I will end your captivity. I will gather you from all the nations and places where I have scattered you, and I will bring you home after your long exile, declares the Lord. (Jeremiah 29:11–14)

In the year 626 BC, when Jeremiah was just a youth, God called him to speak boldly to the Jewish people. Many had turned away from God, pursuing idols, and because of this, God told Jeremiah to warn them that he would remove his protection from his faithless people. He warned that the Babylonians were coming and would take control of the land. If they resisted the Babylonians, Jerusalem and its temple would be destroyed, and the Jewish people would be taken into exile in Babylon.

No one wanted to hear Jeremiah's words. The king and leaders were angry with him. Some of the people wanted to stone him. Meanwhile, Judah's false prophets told a different story, urging the king and his people to resist the Babylonians, trusting that God would deliver the people from the hands of their enemies. Jeremiah was arrested, persecuted, and harassed for calling the people of Jerusalem and their king to repent of their sins and surrender to the Babylonians. But he kept issuing his warnings that Judah would be destroyed if it didn't surrender.

In 597 BC, the Babylonian army plundered Jerusalem, installing a new king and taking many of Judah's leaders to Babylon as captives. After another rebellion eleven years later, Jerusalem was destroyed, just as Jeremiah had predicted.

Jeremiah 29 is a letter to the first group of exiles, written just after they were taken to Babylon in 597 BC. While some were hoping for their speedy return to Judah, Jeremiah tells them to settle in for a long stay. He tells them to build houses, to marry in Babylon, and to "promote the welfare of the city where I have sent you into exile. Pray to the Lord for it, because your future depends on its welfare."

This letter also includes the best-known and most-loved passage in the book, Jeremiah 29:11. Most who quote it don't know its context. Its words are so powerful, they have encouraged countless people in the twenty-six hundred years since Jeremiah penned them. Let's read these words from Jeremiah 29:11–14. If possible, you might even want to read them aloud:

> I know the plans I have in mind for you, declares the Lord; they are plans for peace, not disaster, to give you a future filled with hope. When you call me and come and pray to me, I will listen to you. When you search for me, yes, search for me with all your heart, you will find me. I will be present for you, declares the Lord, and I will end your captivity. I will gather you from all the nations and places where I have scattered you, and I will bring you home after your long exile, declares the Lord.

What do these words, written to exiles who had been taken prisoner to Babylon in 597 BC, have to do with us today? Why are they so often quoted and clung to by people of faith? Because we see in these words a picture of our own lives when things go wrong. And we hear in these words a promise from God, not only for them but for us. God will not abandon us. God hears us when we pray and wishes to give us a future with hope.

God didn't rescue the Jewish people overnight. They lived in exile for decades. But they faced their exile with hope, knowing that God had plans for them, and that these plans, however distant in the future they might be, were plans for peace—they were plans filled with hope.

Seek him, call upon him, and trust him. He has plans to give *you* a future with hope.

Lord, in my moments of exile, the times when I feel alone, afraid, uncertain about the future, help me to trust you. At this moment, I trust my future to you. And I trust that you will rescue me from exile, and that you have plans for me, plans to give me a future with hope.

The Steadfast Love of the Lord

My soul is bereft of peace;
I have forgotten what happiness is;
so I say, "Gone is my glory,
and all that I had hoped for from the Lord."
But this I call to mind,
and therefore I have hope:
The steadfast love of the Lord never ceases,
his mercies never come to an end;
they are new every morning.
    (Lamentations 3:17–18, 21–23a NRSV)

The people did not repent in response to Jeremiah's preaching, or even after the first wave of them were taken into exile. Thus, in the summer of 586 BC,[*] the Babylonian army attacked once more, breached Jerusalem's walls, slaughtered many of its people, burned the pal-

---

[*] There is some debate about whether the year was 586 or 587 BC.

aces, pillaged God's temple, and then burned it to the ground. Jerusalem's king watched as his sons were put to death. Then his eyes were gouged out, making the death of his sons the last thing he would ever see. He and many of the people of Judah were led on a march hundreds of miles long, forced to join the others living in exile in Babylon.

The writer of Lamentations, traditionally believed to be Jeremiah, wrote this five-chapter-long prayer in the aftermath of Jerusalem's destruction.

Fifteen years after 9/11, I walked through the memorial in New York that commemorates that day. The entire museum is deeply moving, but listening to the voices recorded in the midst of that terrible day moved me, literally, to tears. I didn't expect this, not after so many years had passed. It was the reporters attempting to report from the scene, and the recorded transmissions from firefighters and other emergency personnel, and, of course, the cell phone messages from those trapped in the twin towers who were calling to say their good-byes that pierced my heart.

It was in the aftermath of such a crisis, the destruction of Jerusalem and the deaths of thousands of its inhabitants on that summer day in 586 BC, that the author of Lamentations wrote, "My soul is bereft of peace; I have forgotten what happiness is."

People who have never read the Bible often assume that it's a book of platitudes offering a Pollyanna view of a world without suffering. But the opposite is true. Much of the

Bible was written in the face of suffering. The biblical authors were not people who led charmed lives and happily wrote about how good life can be if only you believe in God. No, they were people who faced hardship and pain and who demonstrated a dogged determination to trust in God despite that.

The writer of Lamentations does not bury his head in the sand, pretending that the world is not filled with sorrow. He faces it head-on. His home has been destroyed. He has lost people he loves. He writes, "Gone is my glory, and all that I had hoped for from the Lord."

But note the words that follow these:

But this I call to mind,
and therefore I have hope:
The steadfast love of the Lord never ceases,
his mercies never come to an end. (3:21–23 ESV)

In essence he was saying, "The world may be going to hell, but I count on God's steadfast love." The Hebrew word for "steadfast love" is *chessed.** It means kindness, compassion, mercy. The writer of Lamentations chose to believe that God's mercy, compassion, and love are steadfast, even when the world around him seemed to be crumbling.

---

* You may also see the word spelled as *hessed* or *checed.*

One Sunday, just after worship ended, a family approached me in the foyer. I had not expected to see them in church that morning. Their twenty-six-year-old son had died that week. I hugged them, held them, and then took them into our chapel. The world as they knew it had come crashing down. They didn't blame God; nor were they angry that God had not intervened. They understood that what had led to their son's death was not God's will. They had come to worship that day because God was their only source of hope—hope that they would somehow make it through the terrible darkness, hope that something good could come from their pain, and hope that they would one day see their son again.

God can and will sustain you through the storms that come in life. He will carry you through the grief. And he has a way of wringing good from the tragedies in our lives. When the world is crumbling, we force ourselves to remember that "the steadfast love of the Lord *never* ceases" and "his mercies *never come to an end*."

God, I choose to believe in your steadfast love. I trust in it. I'm counting on it. Help me remember that you are, that you are with me, that you will always be with me, and that, in your mercy and compassion, you will see me through even the darkest of times.

DAY SEVENTEEN

Shadrach, Meshach, and Abednego

[King Nebuchadnezzar said,] "Is it true, Shadrach, Meshach and Abednego, that you do not serve my gods or worship the image of gold I have set up? Now when you hear the sound of the horn, flute, zither, lyre, harp, pipe and all kinds of music, if you are ready to fall down and worship the image I made, very good. But if you do not worship it, you will be thrown immediately into a blazing furnace. Then what god will be able to rescue you from my hand?" (Daniel 3:14–15 NIV)

As we've learned, several years before the destruction of Jerusalem, King Nebuchadnezzar of Babylon took some of the Jewish nobility into exile. Some of these became important servants in the king's palace. Among these were four young men named Daniel, Hananiah, Mishael, and Azariah. An official in the king's court renamed them Belteshazzar, Shadrach, Meshach, and Abednego.

The short Book of Daniel includes two dramatic stories of courage involving these four young men: the familiar story of Daniel being thrown into the lions' den (Daniel 6) and the story of Shadrach, Meshach, and Abednego being thrown into the fiery furnace. I'll leave it to you to read Daniel's story on your own. Let's focus on the story of his three friends.

According to Daniel 3:1, King Nebuchadnezzar erected an image of gold, ninety feet tall and nine feet wide. This idol, which some have likened to an obelisk, likely included an image of one or more of Nebuchadnezzar's gods, perhaps featuring Nebuchadnezzar himself among them. From time to time musicians began to play their instruments, and when they did, anyone near the image was required to bow down in obeisance to the gods. If anyone did not bow down, the king's decree noted, such persons were to be thrown into a fiery furnace.

Shadrach, Meshach, and Abednego, who at the time were high officials in the king's administration, came to see the site, but they refused to bow down to worship. Doing so would have violated the second of the Ten Commandments, which prohibits bowing down before and worshipping idols. They knew the possible consequences of refusing. They would not only lose their jobs, they would lose their lives. Nevertheless, they would not bow to the image.

Powerful men, particularly those who struggle with humility, don't like to have their orders disregarded. When some Babylonians saw that the men refused to bow, they reported it to Nebuchadnezzar, and he became furious. The king brought Shadrach, Meshach, and Abednego before him, questioned them, then ordered them to bow when the instruments sounded or be thrown into the blazing furnace.

I love their reply to the king:

> "King Nebuchadnezzar, we do not need to defend ourselves before you in this matter. If we are thrown into the blazing furnace, the God we serve is able to deliver us from it, and he will deliver us from Your Majesty's hand. But even if he does not, we want you to know, Your Majesty, that we will not serve your gods or worship the image of gold you have set up." (Daniel 3:16–18 NIV)

What courage! The young men must have been terrified, but they refused to compromise their values or faith simply because a powerful king demanded it. They believed that God would somehow save them from the fire, "but even if he does not," they would not bow before the image or serve the king's gods.

I wonder if you've ever been asked to compromise your faith or values under an implied or spoken threat. Plenty of men and women have come to me after being asked to do things they believed were immoral. Some did what they were asked, only to regret it later. Others refused, believing that somehow God would deliver them. Some did, in fact, lose their jobs or face other consequences for their refusal to do what they believed was wrong.

In the case of Shadrach, Meshach, and Abednego, Nebuchadnezzar had the furnace heated seven times hotter than normal, then ordered that the men be bound and thrown into the fire. But listen to what happened next:

> Then King Nebuchadnezzar leaped to his feet in amazement and asked his advisers, "Weren't there three men that we tied up and threw into the fire?" They replied, "Certainly, Your Majesty." He said, "Look! I see four men walking around in the fire, unbound and unharmed, and the fourth looks like a son of the gods." (Daniel 3:24–25 NIV)

How I love this picture of the fourth man in the fiery furnace! Who is this fourth man who "looks like a son of the gods"? Some Jews believe it was an angel of the Lord or a vision of God himself. Many Christians see in this figure in the furnace a prefiguring of Jesus Christ. Both see a picture of a profound spiritual truth: when we resist evil and refuse to compromise our faith or values, God walks with us, even in the fiery furnace of consequences that may come.

Lord, grant me the courage to stand strong when others ask me to do what I know is wrong. Please be with me in the fiery furnaces of life and help me to, like Shadrach, Meshach, and Abednego, trust you with my future, my life, my all.

For Such a Time as This

Mordecai told them to reply to Esther, "Do not think that in the king's palace you will escape any more than all the other Jews. For if you keep silence at such a time as this, relief and deliverance will rise for the Jews from another quarter, but you and your father's family will perish. Who knows? Perhaps you have come to royal dignity for just such a time as this." (Esther 4:12–14 NRSV)

There are so many wonderful stories and scriptures in the Hebrew Bible (the Christian Old Testament) dealing with fear and courage that we don't have time to explore in this short devotional. But we'll consider one last story before moving on to the New Testament: the story of Queen Esther.

The Book of Esther is set sometime around 479 BC, sixty years after the Persians defeated the Babylonians, allowing the Jews to return from exile to their homeland.

Some Jews chose to remain living in what had become the Persian Empire. The story of Esther takes place in the royal city of Susa, where King Xerxes maintained a palace.

Esther is one of only two books in the Bible not to mention God, at least not directly (the other being Song of Solomon). Yet a careful reading of Esther will show that while God is not overtly mentioned, he is at work behind the scenes throughout the story.

The story begins, at least as it relates to Esther, with a fifth-century BC version of ABC's *The Bachelor*. King Xerxes is looking for a new queen, and all the beautiful "bachelorettes" ("virgins" is the term used in Esther) are brought before him, one each day, so that he can choose his favorite. Among the "contestants" brought to Xerxes is the beautiful Esther, who ends up becoming the new queen.

Esther was orphaned as a little girl and raised by her uncle Mordecai. She is very beautiful and, as we will see, cunning and courageous. She is also Jewish, a fact that her uncle Mordecai encourages her to keep under wraps.

Some time later, the king elevates one of his officials, Haman, placing him in charge of all the other officials, and gives orders for all the people to bow down whenever Haman approaches. Esther's uncle Mordecai refuses to bow down before Haman. Knowing that Mordecai is a Jew (but apparently not knowing he is the queen's uncle), Haman responds to Mordecai's slight by asking the king to order the death of all the Jews in the Persian Empire. Tragically, the attempt to destroy the Jewish people has been repeated many times throughout history.

The king, who signs the decree as Haman requested, has no idea that he has signed a death sentence for his own queen, for he doesn't know that she is Jewish. Upon learning of the decree, Mordecai begs Esther to speak to the king in order to save her people. But Esther is afraid. There is a law stating that anyone who approaches the king without first being called by him will be put to death. She hasn't even heard from the king in a month.

It is then that Mordecai challenges Esther not to remain silent in the face of impending genocide, and he offers these famous words to his niece, the queen: "Who knows but that you have come to your royal position *for such a time as this*?" (4:14, NIV, emphasis added).

God may not be mentioned by name in Esther, but again and again there are allusions to the idea that God's unseen hand helps guide some events for his purposes— not everything, but some things. Mordecai suggests that Xerxes's choice of Esther as his queen may not simply have been the result of her good looks and charm but may have been a certain favor God gave her in Xerxes's eyes so that one day she might use her influence for good.

Esther works up her courage, risks everything, and intervenes on behalf of her people. Xerxes grants her request, and the Jewish people are saved from destruction.

I believe that we're each meant to hear Mordecai's

question as directed at us. Who knows but that *you* have come into *your* position of influence and power *for such a time as this*? We each have influence. And there are moments when our influence might play some critical role in ensuring justice for someone else. We can remain silent, because of fear. Or we can use our influence to stand with and for the other. Proverbs calls us to "speak out on behalf of the voiceless, and for the rights of all who are vulnerable" (31:8). This, however, requires moral courage.

When I consider Esther's example, I think of a man I admire, Irv Hockaday. He's a retired president and CEO of Hallmark, the greeting card company, and a thoughtful and committed Christian. In the 1960s, as a young and up-and-coming lawyer and business leader, he was a member of the University Club in Kansas City. The prestigious club had many important business leaders among its members, but no Jewish members. Irv was a director, and he knew this should change, so he nominated a respected Jewish business leader in Kansas City for membership. Anonymous letters came in opposing the man's membership, and the board voted to deny it. But before informing the man that he'd been turned down for membership, Irv submitted his own resignation to the board, an act that could have been costly to his career and future. Within a few years the club changed its policies.

This was the first of many things Irv did across the course of his long and amazing career to "speak out on behalf of the voiceless." He has been, in many ways, an example of moral courage. When he saw injustice, he could hear Mordecai's question: "Who knows? Perhaps your influence was given *for such a time as this?*"

Lord, you know that there are times when I have been too afraid to stand up or to speak out. Please help me use whatever influence you've entrusted to me to "speak out on behalf of the voiceless." Use me to positively shape my community and this world, that it might look more like your kingdom.

God Is Honoring You

God sent the angel Gabriel to Nazareth, a city in Galilee, to a virgin who was engaged to a man named Joseph, a descendant of David's house. The virgin's name was Mary. When the angel came to her, he said, "Rejoice, favored one! The Lord is with you!" She was confused by these words and wondered what kind of greeting this might be. The angel said, "Don't be afraid, Mary. God is honoring you. Look! You will conceive and give birth to a son, and you will name him Jesus. He will be great and he will be called the Son of the Most High." . . . Then Mary said, "I am the Lord's servant. Let it be with me just as you have said." (Luke 1:26b–32a, 38)

ary was a young peasant girl living in the small, seemingly insignificant village called Nazareth. John's Gospel records a moment when the disciple Philip tells his friend Nathaniel that Jesus of Nazareth is the one "about whom the prophets wrote." Nathaniel replies, "Can anything good come out of Nazareth?" This likely summarizes the general disdain with which the village was held by those in Galilee.

One day a stranger came to the village and spoke to Mary. Luke tells us he was the angel Gabriel. Gabriel said to Mary, "Rejoice, favored one! The Lord is with you!" The sudden appearance of this stranger, coupled with his odd greeting, was unnerving to her. Gabriel responded to her anxiety, saying, "Don't be afraid, Mary," for "God is honoring you." He proceeded to tell Mary that she was going to have a child, the long-awaited Messiah.

Shortly after this encounter, Mary traveled to visit her cousin Elizabeth, who was pregnant with a child we know as John the Baptist. Elizabeth immediately told Mary, twice, that she was blessed. In Luke 1, just a few verses after the description of this meeting, Mary is told that she is favored, honored, and blessed.

But God's favor, honor, and blessings are not as we often suppose—they are not a promise of a life of bliss and free of hardship. Just the opposite: his honor, blessings, and favor often involve hardship and sacrifice and adversity. When an angel tells you not to be afraid, be prepared: there might be some *really* frightening things ahead! Consider what lay ahead for Mary:

"Don't be afraid, Mary! God is honoring you!" You are going to have a child out of wedlock. Though he will be conceived by the Holy Spirit, even Joseph will struggle to believe this. Others may shun you as an adulteress or worse.

"Don't be afraid, Mary! God is honoring you!" You will arrive in Joseph's hometown only to find that there is no place for you to give birth. You will give birth as the homeless do, in a stable, and your child's first bed will be a feeding trough for the animals.

"Don't be afraid, Mary! God is honoring you!" You, your husband, and your child will be forced to flee from Bethlehem when the demented King Herod hears about the birth of your child and sends his troops to kill him. You'll travel hundreds of miles along the Sinai Desert until you settle as a refugee in Egypt.

"Don't be afraid, Mary! God is honoring you!" But one day you will watch as your son is nailed to a cross. You'll suffer with him, your heart pierced by the pain.

Gabriel didn't tell Mary all that lay in store for her on that day of the Annunciation in Nazareth. No, Gabriel only told her she was favored and honored, that God was with her, and that she would bear the Christ.

God's path is not for the faint of heart. Likewise, God's favor does not mean a life of ease. There are few blessings in my life that did not include a measure of risk, sacrifice, and occasional adversity. Marriage includes all three, and so does being a parent. Serving as a pastor is a great blessing and honor in my life, *and* it has pierced my heart more times than I can count. The same is true, no doubt, for the blessings you've experienced.

What Gabriel said to Mary, I believe he would say to us today: "The Lord is with you! Don't be afraid."

I love Mary's response to Gabriel that day. Despite her questions and uncertainty, and aware of at least some of the risks, she says to Gabriel, *"I am the Lord's servant. Let it be with me just as you have said."* May you have the courage to make this your prayer when God honors, favors, and calls you. If you do, though the road may be hard, you will find yourself blessed.

Lord, please help me hear your call to take risks, make sacrifices, and do what is inconvenient; help me remember that it is in pursuing these that we find your greatest blessings; and give me the courage to respond to your call with Mary's words: "I am the Lord's servant. Let it be with me just as you have said."

Wrestling with the Devil

Then Jesus was led up by the Spirit into the wilderness to be tempted by the devil. He fasted forty days and forty nights, and afterwards he was famished. The tempter came and said to him, "If you are the Son of God, command these stones to become loaves of bread." (Matthew 4:1–3 NRSV)

The Gospels tell us little about Jesus's childhood. Instead, the real action begins with his baptism at the age of thirty. There the Spirit descends upon him and he hears a voice from heaven saying, *"You are my Son, the Beloved; with you I am well pleased."*

Jesus felt called to minister to the multitudes, to "seek and to save those who are lost" (Luke 19:10). He would lead a revolution, one that began in the human heart but would ultimately lead to God's kingdom coming "on earth as it is in heaven." I believe that Jesus knew, from the start, that he would die for this mission, and that his death would play a key role in the revolution he sought to lead.

But before Jesus began to pursue his mission, he went to pray in the barren, beautiful wilderness of Judea. There the devil came to tempt him. This was the most important wrestling match in history, in which the devil faced his most formidable opponent.

How do you picture this story of the devil tempting Jesus? Did he appear in the wilderness dressed in red spandex tights, carrying a pitchfork, to lead Jesus astray? Or did he come to Jesus as he usually comes to us, sowing silent thoughts that take root in our brains?

I've been tempted by the devil many times, but I've never actually seen him. Instead, I *hear* him. It is like a whisper—not audible but a random thought unleashed in my consciousness. Often the thought seems innocuous at first, though as it gestates, it woos me to think about things I know I shouldn't be thinking about (pride, desire, revenge, etc.), or beckons me to say what I should not say (a harsh reply on social media, a juicy morsel of gossip with friends), or coaxes me to do what I know I should not do.

But most often the ultimate aim of the tempter is not the particular sin you feel drawn to commit. Instead, it is the way in which committing these sins keeps you from accomplishing God's mission in your life or uses you to keep others from experiencing the life God wants them to experience. Temptation, ultimately, is about thwarting God's greater purposes for our lives and the world.

I've personally known a dozen or so pastors who ended up leaving the ministry because of an addiction to alcohol or pornography or gambling, an affair, the desire for riches, or an unhealthy quest for affirmation. In these situations, the devil's great victory was not the particular sin the pastor committed but the ripple of pain and betrayal felt by those affected, the damage done to the credibility of the church, and the years of good that the pastor might have done had they not succumbed.

There's something else to notice about temptation. The devil doesn't need to convince us to commit some great sin to derail us. Sure, murder will land you in prison, adultery can destroy families, and lying will cause you to lose your credibility and more. But sometimes the devil's greatest victories are in making you believe that you will fail, so why even try. Sometimes his knockouts come when he persuades you that you are a nobody who matters to no one— that there is no hope, so why should you go on?

Notice how the first two temptations of Jesus recorded by Matthew begin with the devil whispering these words to Jesus: "*If* you are the Son of God . . ." Did you catch it? At his baptism, Jesus had just heard a voice telling him, "You are my Son, whom I love." He'd come to believe that God was calling him to spend his life in ministry with others, and to be prepared to suffer and die for them. But now a new thought races across his brain: "Am I the Son of God? Did I really hear that voice? Am I really called to spend my life serving others, and to ultimately die for them? Or am I just a carpenter with a Messiah complex?" These questions were intended to stoke a fundamental fear we all wrestle with: the fear of failure.

Turning stones into bread was an invitation to do something absurd—performing magic to prove that he was the Son of God. Jesus refused to play the game, but again, in the wilderness the thought raced across his brain: "*If* you are the Son of God, jump off the highest point of the temple in Jerusalem. If you *really are* the Son of God, he'll not let you fall." The devil's message is clear: "If you aren't the son of God, isn't it better that we end this charade now, and you die from the fall, rather than on a Roman cross?" Once more, Jesus refused to allow the devil to derail him from pursuing God's mission.

The last temptation recorded by Matthew makes more sense to us: "Jesus, if you leave this nonsense of this spiritual revolution, forget about the kingdom, and let someone else pursue the death wish of the cross, you can have all the wealth and power this world has to offer." We see here the fear of missing out. But this temptation was not so different from the first two—it was still an attempt to keep Jesus from pursuing God's mission and from achieving the impact he would have as the crucified king.

Jesus rightly said the devil is the "father of lies." Don't

buy his lies. Don't forget his endgame. And remember, he's not that strong. The scripture promises, "Resist the devil, and he will flee from you" (James 4:7). That's precisely what Jesus did in the wilderness, and what he encourages us to do when we hear the devil whisper.

How grateful I am, O Lord, that you know what it's like to be tempted. You know my struggles. You know my weaknesses, which the devil seeks to exploit. Forgive me for the times I've fallen. Help me to recognize temptation when it comes and to resist and reject the lies of the devil.

A Dangerous, Revolutionary Prayer

[Jesus said to them,] After this manner therefore pray ye:

Our Father which art in heaven, Hallowed be thy name. Thy kingdom come. Thy will be done in earth, as it is in heaven. Give us this day our daily bread. And forgive us our debts, as we forgive our debtors. And lead us not into temptation, but deliver us from evil: For thine is the kingdom, and the power, and the glory, for ever. Amen.
(Matthew 6:9–13 KJV)

Dangerous" and "revolutionary" may not be the words you think of when considering the Lord's Prayer. In fact, when we recite it together in church, it often seems rather innocuous. But early Christians prayed this prayer three times a day, morning, afternoon, and evening, believing it had the power to shape their lives and to change the world.

Let's briefly consider the words Jesus gave us as a pattern for prayer.

Our Father. The very form of this prayer reminds us that we are connected to others; God is *our* Father, not just *my* Father. And despite the truth that God transcends gender, Jesus chooses to speak of God as "Father." In first-century Judaism, the ideal father selflessly sought to guide, care for, protect, and provide for his family. Jesus invites us to see God as one who selflessly guides, cares for, and protects us.

He is our Father, *which art in heaven*. In the time of Christ, heaven didn't simply mean the place we go when we die. Heaven—or, often, the heavens—signified God's entire realm, the vastness of the universe. Yet the Greek word for heaven, *ouranos,* also signifies the atmosphere, even the air we breathe. God's presence fills the universe, yet at the same time is as near as the air we breathe. We see in this one phrase both God's transcendence and God's immanence, God's greatness and God's very nearness to us.

Hallowed be thy name. Thy kingdom come. Thy will be done in earth, as it is in heaven. Two of the first words children learn to say are "my" and "mine." This is why each "thy" or "thine" in the prayer reflects a revolution of the heart. Each of us, by nature, tends to pray, "Hallowed be *my* name. *My* kingdom come, *my* will be done, on earth as

it is in heaven." Our human nature wants the closing dox-
ology of the prayer to be "*Mine* is the kingdom, *mine* is the
power, *mine* is the glory, forever, amen!" But Jesus calls us
to surrender our desire for power and glory and, instead,
seek God's kingdom, power, glory, and will. How radically
different our world would be if the 2.3 billion Christians
on the planet made this the desire of their hearts: "not
mine, but thine."

Give us this day our daily bread. When I pray this prayer
each morning, I'm praying first for those who don't know
where their daily bread will come from. I remember that
God's way of providing for the poor has always been to ask
those who have more than enough to share. My prayer
each day is to be mindful of the poor and to actively look
for ways to share with those in need.

But the prayer also reminds me that, while I have food
enough to spare, "one does not live by bread alone." Jesus
once said, "I am the bread of life. Whoever comes to me
will never go hungry" (John 6:35). I have enough food to
eat, but I need this bread, the living Christ, every day.

And forgive us our debts, as we forgive our debtors. The
Greek word for sin, *hamartia,* used throughout the New
Testament, means to miss the mark. How often we each
miss the mark, falling short of God's path in what we do,
and what we fail to do. Asking for forgiveness was a normal
part of daily prayer. But Jesus changed the prayer—he rev-
olutionized it. We don't simply ask for God to forgive us

but ask that God forgive us "*as we forgive our debtors.*" This is a frightening, dangerous, revolutionary prayer.

And lead us not into temptation, but deliver us from evil. I'm often asked, "Why would we need to pray for God not to lead us into temptation?" James, in his epistle, notes, "No one, when tempted, should say, 'I am being tempted by God'; for God cannot be tempted by evil and he himself tempts no one" (James 1:13). The most satisfying answer to the apparent dilemma was one I heard years ago: "We've put the comma in the wrong place." Huh? Yes. What if Jesus did not intend for us to pray, "Lead us not into temptation" but, instead, wanted us to say, "Lead us, [note the comma] not into temptation"? In essence we are praying, "Lead us, Lord, not into temptation as we so easily lead ourselves. Instead, deliver us from the evil one." When we pray this conclusion to the prayer, we're recognizing our own daily battle with temptation, and we're asking God to lead us, and to lead us away from temptation.

By the beginning of the second century, Christians were praying this prayer three times a day. It beckons us to trust in God as our protector, provider, and parent. It compels us to yield our desire for glory, our longing for our will to be done, to God and God's glory. It invites us to trust in God for all that we need, including forgiveness for our sins. And by it we invite God to lead us in his path. When we really engage in this prayer, when we allow it to shape our hearts, our souls, and our lives, we begin to see that it is, indeed, one of the most revolutionary prayers we can pray.

Our Father which art in heaven, Hallowed be thy name. Thy kingdom come. Thy will be done in earth, as it is in heaven. Give us this day our daily bread. And forgive us our debts, as we forgive our debtors. And lead us, not into temptation, but deliver us from evil: For thine is the kingdom, and the power, and the glory, for ever. Amen.

The Storms at Sea

"By this time the boat, battered by the waves, was far from the land, for the wind was against them. And early in the morning he came walking toward them on the sea. But when the disciples saw him walking on the sea, they were terrified, saying, "It is a ghost!" And they cried out in fear. But immediately Jesus spoke to them and said, "Take heart, it is I; do not be afraid."

Peter answered him, "Lord, if it is you, command me to come to you on the water." He said, "Come." So Peter got out of the boat, started walking on the water, and came toward Jesus. But when he noticed the strong wind, he became frightened, and beginning to sink, he cried out, "Lord, save me!" Jesus immediately reached out his hand and caught him, saying to him, "You of little faith, why did you doubt?" When they got into the boat, the wind ceased. And those in the boat worshipped him, saying, "Truly you are the Son of God." (Matthew 14:24–33)

On my last visit to the Sea of Galilee, a terrible storm woke me up in the middle of the night, with the sound of wind howling through the trees. I stepped outside and tried to imagine how it must have felt when the disciples were caught in such a storm, in the dark in the middle of the lake. It would have been terrifying.

There are two distinct episodes in the Gospels that involve Jesus, the disciples, and storms on the Sea of Galilee. In one story, Jesus was in the boat with the disciples, napping, exhausted, when the storm arose. None of them wanted to bother him, but as the storm intensified, they became frightened. Finally, they woke Jesus, crying, "Lord, help us! We're going to drown!" Sometimes I wonder what they expected him to do. Man an oar? Help with the sail? Whatever it was, it is clear that they were not expecting him to do what he did.

Jesus "got up and gave orders to the winds and the lake, and there was a great calm" (Matthew 8:26). Can you imagine what that must have been like? In awe, the disciples said to one another, "Who is this that even the wind and the waves obey him?"

But the fisherman among them had a clue. There were certain verses from the Psalms that fishermen clung to when the storms came up: Psalms 65:7, 89:9, and 107:25. Each notes that God calms the storms at sea. The disciples were beginning to see that their teacher was no ordinary man!

The second of the storm accounts at sea took place at night. And in this story, Jesus was not in the boat with the disciples. As evening approached, he told them to take the boat and head back to the other side of the lake without him. Normally, it might take an hour for a little boat to cross from one side of the lake to the other (at its widest, the Sea of Galilee is eight miles from east to west). But as the sun set that evening, the winds picked up and shifted. Soon the waves were washing over the bow of the boat, tossing it to and fro.

It was in the midst of the disciples' struggle that Jesus came to them, climbed into the boat with them, and calmed the wind and the waves. The story was not told merely to entertain, or to teach us what Jesus did so long ago. It was intended to teach us that Jesus also comes to *us* in the midst of *our* storms.

As Jesus approached their boat, walking on the water, they cried out in fear, thinking that he was a ghost. In Mark and John's accounts, Jesus climbs into the boat, and the storm immediately calms. I love this image! When you invite Jesus into the boat with you, the storms of fear and anxiety begin to subside.

Matthew adds one detail to the story that Mark and John leave out. While the storm was raging and Jesus was approaching, Simon Peter shouted the most preposterous thing: "If it is really you, Jesus, walking on the water, bid me to join you." Had Peter lost his mind? What kind of request was this? Jesus bade Peter to step out of the boat and join him in the sea. You no doubt know the story. Many of us learned it as children.

Peter stepped out of the boat and began walking on the water toward Jesus. Remarkable! Then a strong wind came up, Peter took his eyes off of Jesus, and he began to sink. He cried out to Jesus, who rescued him. They both climbed into the boat, and the storm subsided.

Why does Matthew include this part of the story? I think it's because he wants us to see that if we focus on the storm instead of the Lord, fear will take us down. But I think he also wants us to know that at times, Jesus invites you to step out of what's safe, comfortable, and easy, to join him on the seas, where the real action is.

As I write these words, a group of men in my congregation are in a Central American country, helping to construct a new wing on a school. Some felt a tinge of anxiety as they left, knowing that the murder rate in this small country is ten times that of the United States; yet still they went, to bless the children in this community. They are among so many in our church who routinely overcome their fears to serve others in places or ways that are unfamiliar or that evoke a bit of anxiety. Why do they do it?

Because they sense Jesus calling them to step outside their comfort zone.

Jesus is in the boat with you. Trust him: it's going to be okay; he's more powerful than the storms. But don't miss this: sometimes he's going to call you to get out of the boat, leaving your comfort zone, taking a risk while keeping your eyes focused on him. And that's where the real adventure begins.

Lord, help me remember that you are with me in the storms. But also help me hear your call when you bid me to step out of the boat and join you on the water. Help me to keep my eyes fixed on you, and to come when you bid me come.

Facing Opposition

Now some of the scribes were sitting there,
questioning in their hearts, "Why does this fellow
speak in this way? It is blasphemy!"
(Mark 2:6–7 NRSV)

When they heard this, all in the synagogue were
filled with rage. They got up, drove him out of the
town, and led him to the brow of the hill on which
their town was built, so that they might hurl him off
the cliff. (Luke 4:28–29 NRSV)

Again the Jewish opposition picked up stones in
order to stone him. (John 10:31)

Many of his disciples turned away and no longer
accompanied him. Jesus asked the Twelve, "Do you
also want to leave?" (John 6:66–67)

From the very start, Jesus faced opposition. When he preached in the little synagogue in his hometown, they turned on him and tried to throw him off a cliff. As he cast out demons, the religious leaders claimed he did so by the power of Satan. When he forgave sins, some accused him of blasphemy. When he hinted at his true identity, they planned to stone him to death.

Matthew summarizes Jesus's ministry with these words: "Jesus traveled among all the cities and villages, teaching in their synagogues, announcing the good news of the kingdom, and healing every disease and every sickness." Many began to follow him. And his popularity made him a threat to the religious leaders. They criticized him behind his back and, increasingly often, to his face. He challenged their interpretation of scripture, their laws, and their hypocrisy. His embrace of those others considered sinners was, for many, a sign that he himself was a sinner.

Some of the things Jesus said were difficult even for his friends and supporters to accept. In John 6:66, a verse number that is easy to remember, we read, "Many of his disciples turned away and no longer accompanied him." Can you feel how painful this must have been to Jesus? We hear it in his voice when, just after this, he turned to the twelve disciples and asked, "Do you also want to leave?"

I don't need to wonder if you've ever been unfairly criticized; I know you have. I know you've had people talk about you behind your back. And I'm confident that you've felt betrayed at some point by someone you considered a friend. The experience is painful, discouraging, and exhausting.

Moses prayed to die after receiving criticism from his fellow Israelites. Jezebel's opposition sent Elijah to the wilderness, praying for the same end. The Book of Psalms is filled with David's laments in the wake of criticism and opposition. And a survey of Saint Paul's letters demonstrates a regular defense of his ministry in the face of criticism that clearly stung, often leveled by his fellow Christians. (For instance, 2 Corinthians 10:10: "For some say [of me], 'His letters are weighty and forceful, but in person he is unimpressive and his speaking amounts to nothing'"! NIV)

One night a politician read to me the cruel letters he'd received. I sat with a schoolteacher ready to quit after her encounters with parents at her first parent-teacher conferences. And I've counseled with dozens of pastors who were ready to throw in the towel after seeing the unkind emails members of their churches had sent their way.

This is part of the price of leadership. If Jesus, Moses, and Paul were criticized as leaders, why would you and I be exempt? At times the criticism is valid; it can be a gift that will strengthen you if you are open to listening and learning. Great leaders don't dismiss criticism out of hand; instead, they consider it, learn from it, and grow through it. But often, as was the case with Jesus, the criticism is not valid and is motivated by jealousy, or insecurity, or someone else's resistance to change. Sometimes they are criticizing you for seeking to do what God has called you to do.

In those cases, Jesus calls us, saying, "Love your enemies and pray for those who harass you" (Matthew 5:44). Saint Paul tells us, "Don't be defeated by evil, but defeat evil with good" (Romans 12:21). We do that, he notes, by practicing kindness toward those who have been unkind to us.

On multiple occasions I've had the opportunity to practice this. Sometimes I have failed. But often, when I've returned kindness to those who've criticized me, I've been surprised to find that it made me feel less discouraged by the criticism. I began to feel empathy for the one who'd lashed out at me. On many occasions, my response of kindness has changed the critic into a friend.

But here's what I don't do: I don't give up simply because I've been criticized. No one ever completed anything worth doing by giving up in the face of opposition. Here's what I think the Lord would say to you today: Criticism will come. Bless the critics, learn from them, but don't give up!

Lord, you know my heart has been hurt by unfair criticism, unkind things said about me, and betrayal. Thank you for reminding me that you experienced far worse than I have. Give me strength to love those who hurt me, and perseverance so that I won't give up.

When Jesus Was Afraid

They went to a place called Gethsemane, and Jesus said to his disciples, "Sit here while I pray." He took Peter, James and John along with him, and he began to be deeply distressed and troubled. "My soul is overwhelmed with sorrow to the point of death," he said to them. "Stay here and keep watch." Going a little farther, he fell to the ground and prayed that if possible the hour might pass from him. "*Abba,* Father," he said, "everything is possible for you. Take this cup from me. Yet not what I will, but what you will." (Mark 14:32–36 NIV)

t is troubling for some to imagine Jesus being afraid. He's the Son of God, so how can he be afraid? But in his time on earth, while Jesus was the Son of God, he was also, the creeds tell us, fully human. To be human is to experience fear. He had the same defense mechanisms as we do, the same fundamental drive to stay alive.

On that Thursday evening of Holy Week, after the supper, Jesus led the disciples to the Mount of Olives, to a place where the olives were pressed. There Jesus went to pray, knowing that at any moment Judas, his betrayer, would arrive with the temple guard to arrest him. The next morning he would be tortured to death by the Roman soldiers.

His brain's amygdala was doing what it was created to do: It was preparing his body to fight or to flee. His heart was beating hard and fast. His breathing had become shallow. His palms were likely sweaty, and his mouth probably dry. His heart and mind were filled with an overwhelming sense of dread, the body's way of motivating a person to act for self-preservation. If you wrestle with panic attacks or anxiety, you know the feelings well.

Listen once more to how Mark describes what Jesus was experiencing: "He began to be deeply distressed and troubled. 'My soul is overwhelmed with sorrow to the point of death.'" Fear was doing what fear is meant to do—it is meant to motivate us to run.

But Jesus didn't run, and he didn't plan to fight. Instead, "he fell to the ground and prayed that if possible the hour might pass from him." He had anticipated his death, from the beginning of his public ministry.

Here, as he wrestled with the path of suffering that lay before him, Jesus prayed, "Take this cup—this cup of pain and suffering—away from me!" Yet, though it was God's own Son who prayed this prayer, God did not take the cup away from him. He strengthened Jesus, walked with him, no doubt agonized with and for him. But Jesus still endured the cross. Ultimately, God did deliver him from death at Easter, using the suffering of Jesus for his saving purposes.

In our lives, too, suffering comes. And we, like Jesus, pray for the cup to pass from us. God strengthens us, walks with us, agonizes with and for us, and ultimately delivers us. And, if we allow him, God will use our suffering, redemptively, in our lives.

Jesus's prayer—"Take this cup from me. *Yet not what I will, but what you will*"—is a pattern of prayer for such moments in our lives. We lay our petition before God, and we yield our will to God's will.

Was it God's will that Jesus be betrayed, arrested, humiliated, and then tortured to death? No! God doesn't will cruelty and inhumanity. God's will was to redeem and save the human race; to unveil on the cross the depth of humanity's moral depravity; to reveal the greatness of God's extravagant mercy; to demonstrate "love's width and length, height and depth" (Ephesians 3:18); and, coupled with the resurrection, to proclaim God's decisive victory over evil, hate, sin, and death. The suffering and death of Christ were the means by which God hoped to save the world, a world that includes me and you.

Suffering will sometimes come in life. Our brains are

designed to protect us from it—fear is the mechanism intended to lead us to fight or flee. Sometimes we can't run from suffering or fight it, but can only endure it. And when that is the case, we pray for God's will to be done through it. He may not have willed the suffering, but he wills to use it redemptively—to force good to come from it.

Father, my suffering is nothing compared with that of your Son. But like him, I pray for the cup to pass from me. If I must endure it, please strengthen me and walk with me. Use the suffering I pass through for your good purposes. I trust that, ultimately, you will deliver me from evil. And may my prayer always be this: Not my will, but thy will be done.

When Courage Fails Us

Then Jesus told them, "This very night you will all
fall away on account of me. . . ." Peter replied, "Even
if all fall away on account of you, I never will."
"Truly I tell you," Jesus answered, "this very night,
before the rooster crows, you will disown me three
times."

But Peter declared, "Even if I have to die with you, I
will never disown you." (Matthew 26:31, 33–35 NIV)

I t was night, and Jesus was leading his disciples from the
Upper Room, where they had shared the Passover Seder.
They were still perplexed by Jesus's words, foretelling his
death. As they walked across the Kidron Valley to the place
of prayer in Gethsemane, Jesus spoke once more: "Tonight,
you will all fall away on account of me."

Can you imagine what this felt like to the disciples?

Once more it was Peter who spoke up: "Even if the rest of them fall away, I never will." That's what I would have wanted to say. Jesus replied, telling Peter, "Before sunrise, you yourself will deny knowing me, *three times*." Peter should have remained quiet. Instead he declared, "Even if I have to die with you, I will never disown you."

The story of Peter's denial of Jesus on the night of Christ's arrest is one of the best-known stories in the Gospels. By the time the Gospels were written, Peter was a hero who had courageously died for his faith, yet he is memorialized in all four Gospels for his greatest failure. That is inconsistent with how we tend to remember our heroes. Usually we downplay their failures and highlight their positive accomplishments.

Elsewhere I've written on Peter's life[*] and have suggested that this story was preserved in the Gospels because Peter himself had preached it again and again in the decades between Easter and his own death. It likely became one of his defining stories, so that the Gospel writers could not speak of Peter without telling this story.

Let's recount the story; then we'll reflect upon why the story has connected with Christians of every age.

After Jesus was arrested in Gethsemane, nine of the

---

[*] See *Simon Peter: Flawed but Faithful Disciple* (Nashville: Abingdon Press, 2018).

disciples fled. But Simon Peter and John, according to John's Gospel, followed at a distance as Jesus was taken to the home of the high priest for trial. Let's give Peter credit here. It took courage for him to enter the courtyard of the high priest's home following the arrest. Some of those in the courtyard had likely been there at the arrest. You may remember that, during the arrest, it was Peter who drew his sword, cutting off the ear of the high priest's servant. Had he been recognized, he could have been arrested, too. It took courage for Peter to stand there in the courtyard.

But his courage eventually failed him. Here's Matthew's version of what happened next: A servant girl spoke to Simon Peter in the courtyard, saying, "You were with Jesus, weren't you?" Reflexively, he lied: "I don't know what you are talking about." Then Peter went to stand by the gate, perhaps thinking he might need to flee. Another woman approached, saying to those standing near, "This man was with Jesus, the man from Nazareth." Peter lied again, this time making a solemn pledge: "I don't know the man." Matthew continues: "A short time later those standing there came and said to Peter, 'You must be one of them. The way you talk gives you away.'" This time "Peter cursed and swore, 'I don't know the man!'" Then the cock crowed. Remembering Jesus's words, Peter "went out and cried uncontrollably."

Can you imagine Peter telling this story as he traveled across the Roman Empire, encouraging Christians and those interested in the faith? My experience as a pastor is that people are far more interested in hearing about the times I've failed than when I've succeeded. These stories humanize the teller, but they also connect with hearers because everyone has failed. In the case of Peter, if he could fail and be forgiven and restored, then there's hope for each of us.

Have you ever denied Christ? Maybe you kept your faith under wraps because you were afraid it might cost you friends. Maybe you should have spoken up when you saw or heard something that was wrong, but you remained silent, afraid of the cost of speaking out. Perhaps you've treated people in ways that were inconsistent with your faith, or you've pursued things that were, by the very doing of them, a denial of your faith in Christ. We've all been Simon Peter in one way or another.

What makes this story compelling is that, after Christ's death and resurrection, Jesus forgave Peter, restored him, and continued to use him, and his biggest failure, to build the church. Sometimes it is our greatest failures that become our most compelling witness to the grace and mercy of God.

Lord, forgive me for the times I've denied you. Forgive me for my failure to speak up, or to be counted as one of your disci-

ples, for fear of what others would think. Forgive me for the moments when I've denied you by my actions. As you restored Simon Peter, I ask that you restore me, and use me for your purposes, that my failures might point others to your amazing grace.

The Seven Last Words of Jesus

Jesus called out with a loud voice, "Father, into your hands I commit my spirit." (Luke 23:46 NIV)

t would have been difficult to speak while hanging from a cross. Doing so would have required pulling yourself up by the nails that pierced your hands or wrists, an act that would have caused excruciating pain. If you managed to say something from a cross, it meant that the words you chose must have been important.

The Gospels record seven statements Jesus made during the six hours of his crucifixion, often referred to as the "seven last words." Each year on Good Friday I pray these words and meditate on their importance as a way of reflecting on Christ's death. Many people have written entire books on these words.*

* My own deeper reflection on these words is found in a Lenten book I wrote some years ago, *Final Words from the Cross* (Nashville: Abingdon Press, 2011).

I invite you to reflect on each of these statements with me today.

"Father, forgive them, for they don't know what they're doing." (Luke 23:34)

Jesus had taught his disciples to forgive others. He taught them to love their enemies and pray for those who persecuted them. It's one thing to say this in a sermon; it is another to practice it from a cross. In doing so, Jesus modeled forgiveness for us, setting an example. But his prayer was also *on our behalf.* He prayed for you, and for me, "Father, forgive them, for they don't know what they're doing." *Thank you, Lord, for your mercy.*

"I assure you that today you will be with me in paradise." (Luke 23:43)

Two bandits—both of them thieves and violent thugs who opposed the Romans—were crucified on either side of Jesus. After hearing Jesus pray for his tormentors, one of these bandits turned to Jesus, saying, "Jesus, remember me when you come into your kingdom." Jesus raised himself by his wrists to speak: "Today you will be with me in paradise." I love this exchange, for it reminds me that no one is ever too far gone to trust in Christ, and to his dying breath, Jesus was seeking to draw sinners to God. *Thank you, Lord, for your love for sinners.*

"Woman, here is your son." "Here is your mother."
(John 19:26–27)

What always strikes me about this line is that while he
was suffering immensely, Jesus was concerned not for himself but for his mother, for her suffering and her future.
Hearing Jesus's concern for his mother reminds me of the
care and concern I'm meant to have for my own parents.
Help me, Lord, to care for my parents.

"My God, my God, why have you forsaken me?"
(Matthew 27:46 and Mark 15:34)

Two of the last seven statements Jesus uttered were
prayers from the Psalms. This statement, the only one
mentioned by Matthew and Mark, comes from Psalm 22:1.
The pathos in this prayer deeply moves me. Jesus *feels* forsaken by God. Yet in the moment when he feels most forsaken, what does Jesus do? He prays. He can't feel God,
but he prays. He doesn't see God's deliverance, but he
prays. There are moments in life when we will feel forsaken
by God. But God has not forsaken us. In those moments,
like Jesus and David before him, we pray. *Lord, when I feel
forsaken, help me to pray and to trust that you have not forsaken me.*

"I am thirsty." (John 19:28)

John nearly always intends a deeper meaning when he includes details that seem superficial. Thirst is a part of dying, and loved ones often help the dying with small amounts of water placed on their tongue. But John is pointing to something deeper. In John 4, Jesus offers a woman "living water," saying, "Whoever drinks from the water that I will give will never be thirsty again." Yet here on the cross, the source of living water is himself parched (see also Psalm 22:15) as his life ebbs away. *Lord, help me to thirst for you and the living water you give.*

"It is finished." (John 19:30 NRSV)

In Greek, "it is finished" is one word, *tetelestai.* I used to hear this statement as a cry of resignation, as if Jesus were saying, "My suffering is over" just as he prepared to breathe his last. But I appreciate Bishop Will Willimon's interpretation: "I am hearing this word as the same word Michelangelo uttered when he put his last touch of paint on the ceiling of the Sistine Chapel."* *Tetelestai* was not a cry of resignation but a shout that this masterpiece of Christ's redemptive work was completed, that his saving mission was accomplished. *Thank you, Lord, for your extravagant love.*

---

* William H. Willimon. *Thank God It's Friday: Encountering the Seven Last Words from the Cross* (Nashville: Abingdon Press, 2006), p. 62, Kindle.

"Father, into your hands I commit my spirit."
(Luke 23:46 NRSV)

In his final words in Luke's Gospel, Jesus once more prays a psalm, this time Psalm 31:5. William Barclay described this verse as one Jewish mothers taught their children to say before they went to bed at night, something like the familiar "Now I lay me down to sleep . . ." There is something deeply moving in imagining Jesus's final prayer from the cross as one his mother had taught him as a little boy. It was a declaration of trust that, at his death, he would be safe in his Father's arms. When you are facing dark moments, when you are feeling all alone, when you are frightened or uncertain about what the future holds, join Jesus in praying this prayer: *Father, into your hands I commit my spirit.*

Lord, your words from the cross move me. Help me to forgive as you forgave. To welcome the lost as you welcomed the bandit. To care for my family as you cared for your mother. And when I feel forsaken, console me with the knowledge that you once felt that way, too. When I'm thirsty, fill me with your living water. Help me to see the masterpiece that was finished on the cross. And with you I pray, "Father, into your hands, I commit my spirit."

DAY TWENTY-SEVEN

Easter

It was still the first day of the week. That evening, while the disciples were behind closed doors because they were afraid of the Jewish authorities, Jesus came and stood among them. He said, "Peace be with you." After he said this, he showed them his hands and his side. When the disciples saw the Lord, they were filled with joy. Jesus said to them again, "Peace be with you." (John 20:19–21)

Jesus died at about three in the afternoon on what we now call Good Friday. Good Friday is only good in hindsight. For any who loved and followed Jesus, the day was most assuredly not good. Jesus's body was removed from the cross and hastily prepared for burial because the Sabbath would begin at sunset, and burial would not be permitted once it had begun. A wealthy man named Joseph, a member of the Jewish ruling council, was sympathetic to Jesus. Joseph made his own family tomb available for Jesus's burial.

Most Jews in the first century believed that the spirit descended to the realm of the dead (Sheol or Hades) after death. The part of Sheol reserved for the spirits of the righteous was called paradise. Jesus had told the bandit on the cross, "Today you will be with me in paradise." But while Jesus's spirit was in the realm of the dead, the disciples were stuck in a living hell. Traumatized and terrified, they went into hiding, likely in the same guest room where they had eaten the Passover Seder with Jesus less than twenty-four hours earlier. The doors were now locked, for fear that the religious authorities might seek to arrest them and finish off the movement Jesus had begun.

Early on Sunday morning, it was the women who had the courage to leave and go to the tomb, hoping that someone might roll back the stone and let them finish the burial ritual left undone on Friday. But upon arriving, they found that the stone had been rolled away and the tomb was empty. An angel told the women that Jesus had been raised from the dead. Shortly after that, Jesus began appearing to his disciples.

"Peace be with you," Jesus said to his disciples that first Easter evening. These words capture the impact of the resurrection on those who saw Christ. Terror and trauma melted away, replaced by *shalom,* or peace, and great joy. It was unthinkable that Jesus, who had been tortured to death, then buried, could be sitting in their midst. He was alive. Theirs was not simply the joy of seeing a deceased loved one again. This was the vindication of everything Jesus had preached and taught and done. It was a powerful proclamation that Jesus, who calmed the wind and the waves, cast out demons, opened the eyes of the blind, who showed mercy to sinners and who brought people to God, was, in fact, Lord. God had come to them in this man. They had felt this, but now they knew.

The liturgy for funeral services in the United Methodist Church begins with various statements of Jesus's, placed together, spelling out the hope Christ offers concerning death:

> Jesus said, "I am the resurrection and the life. Those who believe in me, even though they die, yet shall they live. And whoever lives and believes in me will never die. I am the Alpha and Omega, the beginning and the end, the first and the last. I died, and behold I am alive forevermore. I hold the keys of hell and of death. And because I live, you shall live also."

I have recited these words at the beginning of so many funeral services, I've lost count—the number must be in the hundreds. They are etched in my brain and anchored deep in my soul. I've recited them after the deaths of children, following suicides, after deaths by automobile accident, by illness, murder, and old age. They may seem trite to some. But to me, they are God's response to death, wrapped in a Savior who was crucified, dead and buried: *but on the third day, he rose from the dead.* When we trust in these words, we grieve differently, and we live differently.

Recently, I stopped by a visitation to express condolences to a parishioner whose mother had died. Kim said to me, "I don't feel sad, I feel joy. I keep picturing my mom finally reunited with Dad, and the two of them dancing together. They both had a deep faith, and I know they are safe with Jesus. And that brings me such peace."

Her sense of peace and joy following her mother's death was foreshadowed on that first Easter evening as Jesus said to his disciples, *"Peace be with you."* After he said this, he showed them his hands and his side. When the disciples saw the Lord, they were filled with joy. Jesus said to them again, "Peace be with you."

Lord, help me trust in the amazing story of your triumph over death. Help me live in your peace. And help me live unafraid.

This Little Light of Mine

Jesus came near and spoke to them, "I've received all authority in heaven and on earth. Therefore, go and make disciples of all nations, baptizing them in the name of the Father and of the Son and of the Holy Spirit, teaching them to obey everything that I've commanded you. Look, I myself will be with you every day until the end of this present age." (Matthew 28:18–20)

Luke tells us, "After his suffering, he showed them that he was alive with many convincing proofs. He appeared to them over a period of forty days, speaking to them about God's kingdom" (Acts 1:3). At the end of these forty days, Jesus gave them what Christians call the "Great Commission."

Each of the four Gospels, as well as the Acts of the Apostles, records some version of this commission. These five accounts of the commission have much in common. The church has always understood that this commission was not simply for the earliest apostles but for Christians everywhere and at all times.

Each version of the Great Commission is different, but what follows is my attempt to capture the essential elements of them:

Jesus said to the disciples, "I'll be giving you the Holy Spirit to help you. Now, listen: As the Father has sent me, so I am sending you. Go and be my witnesses throughout the world, sharing the good news with all. Tell them who I am, what I've said, and what I've done. And call everyone to repentance, changing their hearts and lives. Extend to them forgiveness and baptize them. Help them become my disciples and teach them to obey my commands. And I'll be with you every day until the end of the age.*

Here's what I want you to remember today: You are called by Jesus to continue his mission. God sent Jesus to be the light of the world. Jesus called his disciples to reflect his light, to walk in his light, to live his light, and to share

---

* John 20:21–23, Luke 24:44–49, Acts 1:8, Mark 16:15–16, and Matthew 28:18–20.

his light. As we take his light into the world, we push back the darkness.

Every year at our church, we dramatically capture this idea at our Christmas Eve candlelight services. Your church likely does something similar. As they enter, each person is given an unlit candle. Near the end of the service we turn off all the lights, extinguish the altar candles, and remember how dark the world can be at times and how into the darkness of our world, Jesus came, born as a babe in Bethlehem. An individual or family then carries a small lit candle into the room, representing the birth of Christ—one small light coming into the world. We then light the "Christ candle" at the altar.

I remind the congregation that Jesus grew up to be a man who not only said, "I am the light of the world" but who also told his disciples that they are to be light for the world. We remember how he said, "Let your light so shine before others that they might see your good works and give glory to your Father who is in heaven." With that, I light my candle, then I light the candles of others, who then light the candles of others. Row by row, we pass the flame to our neighbors until everyone's candle is lit. When all the candles are burning, we all hold up our candles—and the entire room is filled with light.

This was God's strategy for setting the world aright—bringing light into the world and spreading that light one person at a time. It's also our mission.

This year at Christmas Eve, Bobbi Jo stopped me after the service. Bobbi Jo was once an addict who sold her body to support her habit. Along the way, someone shared the light of Christ with her. As her life turned around, she took the inheritance left to her by her father and purchased an abandoned nursing home in the toughest neighborhood in Kansas City. She renovated it and opened a home for women wishing to leave a life of addiction or just coming out of jail, so that they might have a fighting chance at a new life.

One house turned into a couple of dozen homes. A single person walking in the light became several hundred. This year, a few days before Christmas, residents of those homes pooled their resources and prepared one hundred backpacks for homeless people, each one filled with the kinds of things homeless people need—gloves, hats, food, and more. They went out and delivered these under the bridges and on the streets, the same places where many of these residents used to live. Bobbi Jo described to me the joy they experienced in sharing the light of Christ.

This is your mission, and mine, too. How will you shed his light, walk in his light, and let his light shine through you today?

Every morning right after I wake up, I slip to my knees next to my bed and pray. I thank God for the day, pray for my family members and others on my prayer list, and then

I place my hands, palms up, before myself and pray, saying a prayer like the one that follows. Would you pray it with me now?

Lord, send me on your mission today. Help me to walk in your light, to shine your light, and to share your light with others, that the darkness in our world might be pushed back. Use me today to do whatever you need me to do. In Jesus's name, amen.

Pentecost

When Pentecost Day arrived, they were all together in one place. Suddenly a sound from heaven like the howling of a fierce wind filled the entire house where they were sitting. They saw what seemed to be individual flames of fire alighting on each one of them. They were all filled with the Holy Spirit and began to speak in other languages as the Spirit enabled them to speak. (Acts 2:1–4)

I n the Acts of the Apostles, Luke tells us that before he ascended to heaven, Jesus promised to send the Holy Spirit, who would give the disciples power to be witnesses for Christ in "Jerusalem, Judea, Samaria and to the uttermost parts of the earth"—in other words, to testify to Christ *everywhere*. After Jesus left them, the disciples, now numbering 120 people, waited in Jerusalem, praying for the Spirit to come.

Roughly fifty days after Easter, the Jewish festival of Pentecost (also called the Festival of Weeks and Shavuot) was held to celebrate the spring wheat harvest and commemorate the giving of the Law on Mount Sinai. It was on this day, when Jesus's followers were meeting for prayer, that the Spirit came upon them with the sound of a howling wind and the appearance of fire. They were filled with the power Christ had promised and imbued with the supernatural ability to speak in languages they had not known before. They rushed into the streets and began to "declare the mighty works of God" in the languages of the Jews from across the world who had gathered in Jerusalem.

If the Gospels are the good news about Jesus, the Acts of the Apostles is the good news about the Holy Spirit. When Christians speak of the Holy Spirit, we are referring to God's presence with and within us. On one hand, the Spirit is a power that works in and through us to fulfill Christ's Great Commission. But the Spirit is not just an impersonal power. Jesus described the Spirit as the *parakletos*—this Greek word means "one who comes alongside" as a helper, a companion, an advocate, or a comforter. And the Spirit is not just any spirit but God's Spirit, God's presence at work in us.

The Holy Spirit draws us to God, leads us as we seek to follow Christ, equips us with gifts, and empowers us with boldness. The Spirit nudges us and prompts us as we seek to do God's will each day. If we are to live unafraid, the Holy Spirit must play a key part in our lives. The Spirit filled Peter and the other disciples, who had been hiding in fear of arrest and persecution, with the courage to take their faith to the streets.

I want to live a Spirit-filled, Spirit-empowered, and Spirit-led life. Each morning I invite the Holy Spirit to fill me, shape me, guide me, and lead me. Throughout the day I seek to pay attention to the Spirit's leading and prompting. And as I do, I often find myself in the middle of some conversation or situation where it feels like God needs me or wishes to use me. The key is being open to the Spirit and paying attention.

Recently, something happened as I left the last of five worship services for the weekend. I was tired and ready to go home, where I knew my wife, LaVon, had dinner waiting on the table. But as I walked through the sanctuary, ready to pick up my coat and keys, I heard a whisper—a nudge from the Spirit: "Turn around."

I stopped, turned around, and noticed a woman sitting alone under the balcony—one of the last people left in the room after the service. From where I stood, it looked like she might be on her phone, so I turned away and continued to walk out. But then I felt another nudge, this one saying, "Go back and check on her." When I feel these nudges, I've learned to pay attention.

When I walked back to where the woman sat, I realized that she was praying. It was clear that she'd been crying, too. I sat down near her and gently said, "Would you like to talk?" She opened her eyes, surprised to see me there, but she shook her head no. I asked, "Would it be okay if I prayed for you?" She nodded yes. I took her hand in mine.

I wasn't sure what I was praying for, but I knew that God knew. When I finished, I felt prompted to tell her why I'd come over.

"I was walking in the opposite direction, leaving church. But I felt the Spirit nudge me to turn around—that's when I saw you," I said. "I felt God wanted me to come back to check on you. Is it possible that he sent me back here to let you know that he sees you, he loves you, and he is with you in the midst of whatever you are walking through?"

She didn't want to talk, but I sensed that she, too, felt that our short exchange was an expression of God's care. These kinds of experiences happen frequently when we invite the Spirit to lead us.

As I've written these devotions, I've prayed that the Holy Spirit would speak through me to encourage you. And I believe there are ways the Spirit will use you, too, if you're paying attention. Have you invited the Holy Spirit to fill you, work in you, empower you, and use you today? Why not do so right now?

Come, Holy Spirit. Fill me with your presence and your power. Grant me courage and boldness and help me live unafraid. Please guide me, lead me, form me, and shape me. Help me pay attention to your nudges, so that I might do your work.

In Every Situation

I've been beaten more times than I can count. I've
faced death many times. I received the "forty lashes
minus one" from the Jews five times. I was beaten
with rods three times. I was stoned once. I was
shipwrecked three times. . . . I faced these dangers
with hard work and heavy labor, many sleepless
nights, hunger and thirst, often without food, and
in the cold without enough clothes.
(2 Corinthians 11:23c–27)

F ollowing the day of Pentecost and the outpouring
of the Spirit, the disciples kept preaching on the
streets and at the temple. Thousands came to believe that Jesus was, in fact, the Messiah of God. This
didn't go unnoticed by the religious leaders, the same ones
who'd had Jesus sentenced to die only a couple of months
earlier. The disciples were brought before the leaders and
commanded to stop what they were doing. They were even

beaten in order to persuade them to stop. But the disciples refused to keep quiet.

A young, ambitious Pharisee named Saul (his Greek name was Paul) volunteered to silence these followers of Jesus by arresting them, imprisoning them, and, if necessary, putting them to death for the crime of blasphemy. But soon, in a dramatic conversion story, Saul himself became a believer in Jesus (see Acts 9:1–31).

About 60 percent of the Acts of the Apostles tells the story of Paul's dramatic ministry, in which he took the Gospel to non-Jews throughout the Roman Empire. Along the way he was arrested, beaten, imprisoned, shipwrecked, and ultimately beheaded for his faith. Today's verses come from 2 Corinthians, in which Paul recounts what he'd experienced up to that point in his ministry.

If anyone had reason to give up, it was Paul. He's a perfect example of what I've noted previously: that living "unafraid" means pursuing the life God intends despite our fears, not because we don't feel fear at all.

In Acts 16, Paul and his friend Silas had been preaching in the city of Philippi, in what is today Greece, when the authorities arrested them for preaching customs "Romans can't accept or practice." They were subsequently stripped naked and severely beaten with rods, then thrown into the innermost cell of the town prison. It would be easy to understand if, that night in their cell, Paul and Silas asked

DAY THIRTY: *In Every Situation*

why God would allow them to endure such suffering when they were seeking to do God's work. But that is not what they did. Instead, Acts tells us, they sang hymns to God. And it was in the midst of their singing that an earthquake struck, the prison doors flew up, and their shackles came loose.

Several years later, Paul would write a letter to the believers in Philippi, this time from another prison cell. There, as he awaited possible execution, Paul penned these words to the Philippian Christians:

> Do not worry about anything, but in everything by prayer and supplication with thanksgiving let your requests be made known to God. And the peace of God, which surpasses all understanding, will guard your hearts and your minds in Christ Jesus.
> (Philippians 4:6–7 NRSV)

How does Paul propose we live without worry? By praying continually, laying our concerns before God, and giving thanks in every situation.

When I think about Paul's approach to adversity, a woman named Nancy Brown comes to mind. I've had the honor of serving as Nancy's pastor for the last twenty-eight years, and she has inspired me in more ways than I can count. Her passion has been in serving people facing extreme poverty—and mobilizing people and resources to have a lasting impact for good. I've traveled with her as a part of our mission teams all over the world.

This year, Nancy's cancer returned, but it did not stop her from leading a team of ten women to Zambia, where she is known as "Mama Nancy" for her work in caring for orphans. She's helped create fish ponds, a school, and a feeding program there. And this is but one of a dozen places in the developing world where she's left an enduring legacy of bringing hope to people in harrowing situations. In her Christmas letter, she sounded Paul's note: "It has not been an easy year, but it has been a year of gratitude."

In the face of the unsettling, anxiety-producing situations in life, remember Paul's perspective on death, entrust your life to Christ, and spend as much time as you can giving thanks for all the blessings. These were his keys to finding peace.

Lord, you know my fears and the anxiety-inducing situations in my life. I entrust them, and I trust my very life, to you. I thank you for all of the blessings in my life. Hear me now as I recount them to you, and as I do, grant me the peace that surpasses all understanding . . .

How the Story Ends

Then I saw a new heaven and a new earth, for the former heaven and the former earth had passed away, and the sea was no more. I saw the holy city, New Jerusalem, coming down out of heaven from God, made ready as a bride beautifully dressed for her husband. I heard a loud voice from the throne say, "Look! God's dwelling is here with humankind. He will dwell with them, and they will be his peoples. God himself will be with them as their God. He will wipe away every tear from their eyes. Death will be no more. There will be no mourning, crying, or pain anymore, for the former things have passed away." (Revelation 21:1–4)

The Book of Revelation is one of the most misunderstood and misused books in the entire Bible. Some in the early church didn't count it among the apostolic books. Even as late as the Protestant Reformation, Luther himself had questions about it.

Revelation is often read as a road map to the end times, which is understandable, given the way it is written. This leaves some interpreters looking at the news to find events that might correlate to the odd visions the writer of Revelation describes. Throughout history there have been many who saw in Revelation the events of their own time and therefore were certain that they were living in the end times, only to be disappointed that Christ did not return and put an end to the evil world around them.

It is better, many believe, to see Revelation for what it was: a letter to seven churches in Asia Minor (modern-day Turkey) written in a popular literary style of the time, a style typically referred to as "apocalyptic." Its aim was not to foretell events in the twenty-first century but to use symbolic language to speak about the events happening in the late first century—and, through this language, to encourage early Christians to remain steadfast in their faith.

In Revelation, the Roman Empire is pictured as a prostitute who sits on a seven-headed beast (Rome is "the city on seven hills"). But she will ultimately be destroyed. Therefore, Revelation urges, remain steadfast and don't succumb to her temptations, and don't get discouraged in the face of her hostility. The beast and the woman who sits upon it will be destroyed, and those who persevere in their faith to the end will be saved.

That message is relevant in every age, not as a road map to the end times but as a message of encouragement to faithfulness no matter what. It reminds us that every kingdom and every empire and every nation will ultimately fall, except the kingdom of God. And those who suffer for their faith will have a special honored place in that kingdom. The book's message is powerfully summarized in Revelation 11:15, a verse made even more memorable by Handel's musical arrangement in the "Hallelujah Chorus": *The kingdoms of this world are become the kingdoms of our Lord, and of his Christ; and he shall reign for ever and ever* (KJV).

My wife, LaVon, has an interesting way of reading novels. She reads the opening pages of the book, just far enough to get a basic picture of the story line and the characters. Then, before reading any further, she skips ahead and reads the closing pages of the book. "Why," I once asked her, "do you do this? It seems an odd way to read a book." She smiled and said, "I need to know how it ends, so I'm prepared. I want to know if it is a happy ending or a sad ending, and knowing what happens in the end alleviates some of the stress and anxiety as I read the rest of the story."

That's the role Revelation plays in the Bible and in the life of faith. We turn to this enigmatic book to know how the story ends. There we read of Christ's defeat of the forces of evil, and of death itself. We see that the paradise that was lost in the Bible's opening scene is, in the end, restored and that on that day, *"God himself will be with them as their God. He will wipe away every tear from their eyes. Death will be no more. There will be no mourning, crying, or pain anymore, for the former things have passed away."* How I savor this beautiful picture of what lies ahead for us. Like LaVon's reading of novels, we turn to the Bible's closing story and learn that, no matter what happens today, or tomorrow, our story as human beings ends well. It ends with joy and hope, comfort and peace.

I'm often asked what heaven is like. Surprisingly, the Bible tells us very little about it. But in several places we're told it will be like a wedding banquet or a great feast. Psalm 23 speaks of God preparing a table before us. Isaiah 25 speaks of the climax of history as "a rich feast, a feast with choice wines." Jesus said, "The kingdom of heaven is like a king who prepared a wedding party for his son." In Revelation, as the end of the world draws near, a great crowd cries out, "Let us rejoice and celebrate, and give him the glory, for the wedding day of the Lamb has come."

This image of heaven as a wedding banquet became more powerful for me the night our oldest daughter married. We had the joy of preparing a wedding reception for her and her husband. Following their wedding, friends and family gathered at the reception hall, where we ate together, we toasted and laughed, and we danced together. After the last guest left late that night, LaVon and I collapsed into bed and she turned to me and said, "That was one of the best nights of our lives."

That's how the Bible pictures heaven, as a wedding feast. That's why, no matter how frightening, dark, or discouraging the world may seem, we live with hope. We've read the end of the book, and we know how the story ends—in a dance, a feast, at a place where darkness is vanquished forever. Hallelujah! Amen!

Lord, help me trust in you and in the ultimate defeat of evil and the triumph of love and light and life. I look forward to that day when there is no more sorrow or crying or pain, where all is made new. But in the meantime, help me live my life by faith, with confidence and hope in your unfailing love. I entrust my life to you. In Jesus's name and for his sake, amen.

About the Author

Reverend Adam Hamilton is the senior pastor of the 20,000-member Church of the Resurrection, Kansas City, the largest and most influential United Methodist congregation in the United States. He is a leading voice for reconciliation and church renewal in mainstream Christianity, and the author of more than twenty-five books. His recent releases include *Unafraid: Living with Courage and Hope in Uncertain Times, Making Sense of the Bible, Creed: What Christians Believe and Why,* and *Moses: In the Footsteps of the Reluctant Prophet.*

The recipient of numerous awards and honorary degrees, Adam earned his master of divinity degree at Perkins School of Theology at Southern Methodist University, where he received the B'nai B'rith Award in Social Ethics. He graduated with honors from Oral Roberts University with a degree in pastoral ministry. Since 2010, he has spoken to more than 70,000 Christian leaders in forty states on leadership and strategies for missional outreach.

Adam and his wife, LaVon, have two grown daughters and live in Leawood, Kansas.

ADAMHAMILTON.COM
COR.ORG
FACEBOOK.COM/PASTORADAMHAMILTON
TWITTER: @REVADAMHAMILTON

About the Type

This book was set in Galliard, a typeface designed in 1978 by Matthew Carter (b. 1937) for the Mergenthaler Linotype Company. Galliard is based on the sixteenth-century typefaces of Robert Granjon (1513–89).